Key Concepts in
Radio Studies

Recent volumes include:

Fifty Key Concepts in Gender Studies
Jane Pilcher and Imelda Whelehan

Key Concepts in Medical Sociology
Jonathan Gabe, Mike Bury and Mary
Ann Elston

Key Concepts in Leisure Studies
David Harris

**Key Concepts in Critical Social
Theory**
Nick Crossley

Key Concepts in Urban Studies
Mark Gottdiener and Leslie Budd

Key Concepts in Mental Health
David Pilgrim

**Key Concepts in Journalism
Studies**
Bob Franklin, Martin Hamer, Mark
Hanna, Marie Kinsey and John
Richardson

**Key Concepts in Political
Communication**
Darren G. Lilleker

**Key Concepts in Teaching Primary
Mathematics**
Derek Haylock

Key Concepts in Work
Paul Blyton and Jean Jenkins

Key Concepts in Nursing
Edited by Elizabeth
Mason-Whitehead, Annette
McIntosh, Ann Bryan,
Tom Mason

**Key Concepts in Childhood
Studies**
Allison James and Adrian James

**Key Concepts in Public
Relations**
Bob Franklin, Mike Hogan,
Quentin Langley, Nick Mosdell
and Elliot Pill

The SAGE Key Concepts series provides students with accessible and authoritative knowledge of the essential topics in a variety of disciplines. Cross-referenced throughout, the format encourages critical evaluation through understanding. Written by experienced and respected academics, the books are indispensable study aids and guides to comprehension.

HUGH CHIGNELL

Key Concepts in
Radio Studies

Los Angeles • London • New Delhi • Singapore • Washington DC

First published 2009

Apart from any fair dealing for the purposes of research or
private study, or criticism or review, as permitted under the
Copyright, Designs and Patents Act, 1988, this publication
may be reproduced, stored or transmitted in any form, or by
any means, only with the prior permission in writing of the
publishers, or in the case of reprographic reproduction, in
accordance with the terms of licences issued by the Copyright
Licensing Agency. Enquiries concerning reproduction outside
those terms should be sent to the publishers.

SAGE Publications Ltd
1 Oliver's Yard
55 City Road
London EC1Y 1SP

SAGE Publications Inc.
2455 Teller Road
Thousand Oaks, California 91320

SAGE Publications India Pvt Ltd
B 1/I 1 Mohan Cooperative Industrial Area
Mathura Road
New Delhi 110 044

SAGE Publications Asia-Pacific Pte Ltd
33 Pekin Street #02-01
Far East Square
Singapore 048763

Library of Congress Control Number: 2008929909

British Library Cataloguing in Publication data

A catalogue record for this book is available from the
British Library

ISBN 978-1-4129-3516-6
ISBN 978-1-4129-3517-3 (pbk)

Typeset by C&M Digitals (P) Ltd, Chennai, India
Printed in India at Replika Press Pvt Ltd
Printed on paper from sustainable resources

contents

Introduction   1

Part I   Genres and Production   **5**

Acoustics   7
Broadcast Talk   9
Comedy   13
DJs and Presenters   17
Documentaries and Features   22
Drama   26
Magazines   30
Music   33
Phone-ins   37
Podcasting   41
Recording   44
Serials and Soaps   48
Sport   52
Talk Radio   56

Part II   Audiences and Reception   **61**

Audience   63
Blindness   67
Codes   71
Co-presence   74
Hot and Cool Media   78
Imagined Community   81
Intimacy   85
Liveness   87
Noise   91
Radiogenic   93
Radio World   95
Reception   97
Secondariness   99
Sound Culture   103
Soundscape   105

contents

v

Part III   The Radio Industry   109

Advertising   111
Commercialism   114
Community Radio   118
Convergence   122
Formats   125
Internet Radio   127
Localism   131
Micro Radio   134
Pirate Radio   137
Regulation   140
Transmission   145

Part IV   Politics and the Public Sphere   149

Current Affairs   151
Development   155
Gender   157
Hate Radio   161
Journalism   164
News   166
Politics and the Public Sphere   171
Propaganda   175
Public Service Broadcasting   178
Radiocracy   183

References   186

Introduction

This is a book about radio and the relatively new subject of radio studies. In fact, it is the first book to have the words 'radio studies' in its title. Radio itself has been the subject of research and writing since it was invented at the beginning of the last century. Much of that published work concerns the technical dimension of radio, but there is also a significant body of work on, for example, radio history, on the nature of speech on radio, on radio drama and so on. This body of writing is fairly puny in comparison with the literature on film and television but it is important nonetheless. Turning to the slightly more introspective aspect of this book, the consideration of radio studies itself, the published literature is almost non-existent. Very few writers have turned their attention to the nature of this subdivision of media or communication studies and I hope that what follows will take a step in that direction.

There are many reasons why radio has been neglected in media studies, at least in British academic life. Media studies was principally the creation of the Centre for Contemporary Cultural Studies at Birmingham University under their director, Stuart Hall. As Scannell explains, 'work in the centre explored the press, radio and television, but the last of this trio received most attention, because it had become, in the 1960s, the most popular everyday source of entertainment and political information and debate for most British people' (2007: 199). Some of the most influential research carried out in the centre was on television, for example the study of the television programme *Nationwide* and the detailed analysis of one edition of the current affairs programme *Panorama* (Scannell, 2007: 212). Hall's colleagues and students went on to dominate media studies in the UK, but as scholars of visual media and especially television, little wonder radio was temporarily neglected. The state of radio studies in America appears to be a lot healthier and I discuss below some of the American influences on this book. There is a tradition of studying American radio which goes back to the pre-war era; a good example is the work of the Princeton Office of Radio Research which published Hadley Cantril's study of Orson Welles's famous broadcast, *War of the Worlds*, and its remarkable public reception.

It used to be the case that books about radio would begin with a rather apologetic justification for writing about the 'neglected' medium.

We lived in a visual culture, television was dominant, radio was ignored but should not be. It is certainly true that radio was ignored; books on the media were often in reality books on television, the importance of radio drama was ignored, as was radio news and current affairs. 'The media' was in fact shorthand for 'the visual media'. The situation today is rather different. There will be no justification here for a book about radio because none is needed. Radio, and here I mean not just broadcast analogue radio but digital radio, Internet radio and podcasts, has asserted itself to such a degree that excuses are unnecessary. Some readers might think that I am stretching the term radio to include audio and indeed the new technologies of the Internet and podcasting. I think this is splitting hairs. No medium can be defined by the technology of its delivery: a podcast remains radio because of the way it is produced. A film, after all, is still a film even when it is shot using a digital video camera and watched on a television set.

In writing this book I have made the rather presumptuous claim that there are central concepts used in radio studies. This is open to question: there is no agreed conceptual framework for a subject area in such an early stage of development. My choice of concepts barely reflects common usage but instead is an attempt to list and describe what seem to me to be some useful and often used ideas and terms. A different author would have produced a different selection of concepts and for that reason I need to explain the thinking behind my own.

The concepts chosen here are derived from two sources. The first source is the business of producing radio itself; this includes the genres and styles of programming (the phone-in, news, comedy and so on) and other central ideas and practices of the radio industry (for example the radio format, the audience, radio journalism). These are terms which are used in the radio industry itself and so have a professional currency. The second source for my list comes from writing about radio from within the academic field of media studies, including radio studies. So, for example, the idea that radio is an 'intimate' medium is a recurrent theme in the radio studies literature, as is the 'liveness' of radio and the idea of the radio DJ's 'persona'. These are not terms, however, often used in the radio industry but belong to the critical discourse about the medium which tries to make sense of it from the outside. In addition there are a few concepts here which are not radio specific; the concept of the 'imagined community' was not developed with radio in mind but appears in a number of books on the subject. Other examples in this category are public service broadcasting, propaganda and development and

I would argue that adding a radio perspective to these topics adds to our understanding of the media more generally. Finally, I have also added some concepts which have barely been written about at all but which seem to me to be full of potential for radio studies: I have used what might in other circumstances be called 'poetic licence'. There is no consensus about what terms like 'radiogenic', 'radiocracy' and 'radio world' mean, but they are clearly useful concepts and I have made a rash attempt to define them and explain why they are important.

My approach to writing the individual entries also needs some justification. There are two main influences here: first, my own interest in radio history; and, second, the belief that it helps our understanding of radio to consider the British and American experience at the same time. Most of the entries include some sort of historical context which includes 20th-century examples if they help us to understand radio today. As for the use of both American and British examples and experiences, my reasons for this transatlantic approach are partly intellectual and partly personal. I would argue that in almost every aspect of the medium we can understand it better if we study both sides of the Atlantic. So regulation, the DJ, the localness of radio – an understanding of all of these is so much more complete if both the American and the British traditions are considered. These two national examples are sufficiently different and sufficiently similar to make comparison rewarding and, as previously mentioned, there is a strong tradition of radio scholarship in America which has produced a significant literature. My other reason for acknowledging the American case is that I am a member of the 'baby boomer' generation which grew up at the height of American cultural influence on Britain in the 1950s and 1960s. Jack Kerouac, Ken Kesey, The Grateful Dead, these were my cultural influences and so when I started the research for this book I found myself turning to the two most important cultural histories of US radio, Michele Hilmes's *Radio Voices* and Susan Douglas's *Listening In*. Both of these sources, together with Christopher Sterling's excellent *Encyclopedia of Radio*, are widely used here and indeed made this book possible. I should add here the continued importance and influence of Andrew Crisell's ground-breaking book *Understanding Radio*, first published almost quarter of a century ago. There are repeated references to Crisell's book here and, like him, I have tried to write about the 'distinctive characteristics of the radio medium' (Crisell, 1986: xv).

Radio is a remarkable subject for students and scholars alike. There is something incurably fascinating about the oldest broadcasting medium.

Once the only form of broadcasting, then the victim of television's success, reprieved as the natural voice of popular music and youth culture and now on the crest of the wave of more democratic, user-generated forms of audio, radio seems to be both ancient and modern; so yesterday and yet so tomorrow. In our visual culture, radio persists without pictures as the 'blind' medium but in this invisibility it retains a special power to communicate. Important, even dominant, though the visual is, sound communication through chat, the phone, in music and on radio remains both different and extremely important. We no longer live in oral societies where all communication and knowledge was through speech, but we do live in the age of 'secondary orality' (Ong, 1988) where the electronic media, including radio, thrives on the immediate and intimate qualities of speech and sound. This book reflects and even celebrates radio's unique and somehow irrepressible voice.

Cross-reference to other entries in the book are **emboldened**.

Hugh Chignell
The Media School, Bournemouth University
August 2008

Part I
Genres and
Production

Acoustics

> **Acoustics refers to the quality and nature of sound in a particular physical environment. It also refers more generally to sound and hearing as in 'acoustic dislocation'.**

The word acoustics is used in two rather different ways in writing on radio. It has a specific technical meaning in radio production, which refers to either natural sound qualities of different locations or to their treatment. This use of the word acoustics is usually seen in discussion of radio drama. It is also used, however, in a much more general way to refer to sound production and hearing and especially in cultural or historical accounts of sound.

In radio production, and in particular on location, the sound quality of the environment is an important factor. This is partly determined by the reflective properties of surfaces and their distance from the microphone (Starkey, 2004a: 11). In reflective environments, sound bounces off hard surfaces to create an echo or 'reverberation' or 'resonance'. Lobbies or toilets cause high levels of reverberation and so does a church or a hall where the greater space creates a slower echo. In drama production these effects are either achieved on location or are created artificially in the studio to add atmosphere to the drama. Acoustics allow the listener to 'hear space' or, to put it differently, 'space is created acoustically' (Shingler and Wieringa, 1998: 56). These sound qualities add something to the listener's experience:

> If the sounds are produced in a studio and all resonance is deadened then these sounds seem to occupy the same space as that of the listener, replicating the acoustic qualities of most people's homes, where typically sounds are deadened by carpets, wallpaper, curtains and furniture. (Shingler and Wieringa, 1998: 56)

Here the acoustic deadening of the studio is used to enhance the intimacy of the listening experience and the simulation of co-presence between the presenter or DJ and the listener.

The other use of the word acoustic is found in cultural and historical accounts of listening. Emily Thompson's (2004) history of sound and technology in the early 20th century is entitled *The Soundscape of Modernity: Architectural acoustics and the culture of listening in America, 1900–1933*. The book is not directly concerned with radio but looks at the wider soundscape of modern America, its 'aural landscape'. She comments on the way that in the noisy urban environment of the American city, acoustic technology was used in architecture and building materials to try to reduce the din of modern technology (trains, cars, gramophones). Gradually, 'electroacoustic' devices such as the telephone and the radio changed the listening experience and gave the listener greater control over what they heard. A feature of the new listening was that 'sound was gradually dissociated from space' (Thompson 2004: 2). So the telephone conversation separated the human voice from their location. Similarly, radio allowed voices, some of them from other countries, to speak into enthusiasts' headphones.

Returning to the word 'acoustic' we can say that the acoustic experience has historically moved in the direction of both *control* over what is heard but also in the *separation* of sound and place. This is a point made not only by cultural historians but also in contemporary cultural accounts of audio consumption. Personalised audio players (such as the Walkman® or its replacement, the MP3 player) contribute to the acoustic experience in ways very similar to those described by Thompson:

> … listening with headphones on is like a wonderful decoding instrument of the urban sonic environment. The walking listener uses it not only to protect himself from the sonic aggressions of the city but also to filter and enhance the events that give the place its meaning. (Thibaud, 2003: 330)

In this case the older technology of the Walkman® audio cassette player is used to screen out unwanted sound and replace it with selective listening, 'the passer-by with headphones navigates through several worlds at once, the one in which he hears and the one in which he walks' (Thibaud, 2003: 331). The acoustic dislocation of the listener from their physical place is also a feature of mobile phone use. Here the acoustic experience seems to lift the user out of the urban environment to other places, 'I am no longer embedded in my immediate locality' comments Caroline Bassett on her phone use, 'today the city streets are full of virtual doorways, opening into other places' (2003: 345).

The idea of acoustics and the related concept of the soundscape are particularly useful for an understanding of contemporary radio. They force us to connect radio to other modes and technologies of listening and to acknowledge both the historical and cultural influences on our sense of hearing.

FURTHER READING

Shingler and Wieringa provide a very useful introduction to this and related topics (1998: 54–61). Thompson's (2004) history of American audio life is fascinating while Thibaud (2003) is a more contemporary account.

Broadcast Talk

> **Broadcast talk refers to talk on radio as a specific form of public broadcast speech.**

It would be hard to exaggerate the importance of talk on radio. In the same way that visual images (or pictures) are fundamental to film and television, so talk is often described as the 'primary code' of radio. This may even be true in music radio where the linking words of the DJ are of critical importance and make the output 'radio' rather than just a jukebox.

But what exactly is 'talk'? Is it the same as language? In addition, what is 'broadcast talk'? Is that the same essentially as 'ordinary talk', which just happens to be transmitted over the radio? The answer to the first question is clearly that language is a resource with its own rules, vocabulary and grammar that can be used in a number of different forms of 'talk'. So the English language can be used in the formal context of the courtroom but this is quite different from the informality of talk in the playground or on the street. In the context of radio theory, 'talk' is used to refer to use of language (vocabulary and grammar) but also mode of address (including 'direct address' which uses 'you', 'we', 'I' and so on). It also includes the sound of someone talking, so accent, noise levels and the rapidity of speech are all included. But 'broadcast talk' is clearly different again from everyday conversational talk. What we hear on the radio in the exchanges between a presenter and someone phoning in, or in the chat of the DJ, or between co-presenters, has a number of largely hidden but distinct characteristics. What we hear *sounds like* everyday talk but is in fact quite different.

To begin with, broadcast talk (a term normally associated with the work of Paddy Scannell [1991]) is meant to be overheard. This is obvious in the direct address of the presenter or DJ who speaks directly to the listener, but it is also true of the talk we hear between the presenter and others involved in the programme, including listeners who have phoned in. Scannell used the term 'double articulation' to describe this characteristic of broadcast talk; there are two simultaneous forms of communication occurring, that between the presenter and the person they are talking to and also between this talk and the audience. So it sounds like 'chat' but it is chat that is designed for thousands of listeners to hear. There is an important tension here between what radio sounds like to the casual listener and a deeper reality. The reality is that the radio station and the presenter have, more or less, complete control or power over what is heard and said. As Scannell puts it, 'the power of broadcasting, like that of any institution, lies in the way it can define the terms of social interaction in its own domain by pre-allocating social roles and statuses, and by controlling the content, style and duration of its events' (1991: 2). This institutional authority is illustrated by the fact that so much of the apparently casual banter that we hear on radio is either scripted or rehearsed. First, jokes, asides, topics, exchanges may have been rehearsed beforehand and are written down in front of the presenter. Second, callers to phone-in programmes are always carefully screened and when they say what they are not supposed to say are quickly cut off.

Broadcast talk may be institutional and contrived but it must sound very different. In the case of the DJ or the phone-in host, quite an effort is necessary to sound spontaneous and everyday. Despite the size of the audience and the pre-planned nature of the talk, the presenter has to perform 'being ordinary' and their speech has to sound much more like everyday conversation than something being read. In Britain there is an interesting and well-documented history of the development of broadcast talk. The first Director of Talks in the BBC, Hilda Matheson, was one of the first to understand the importance of making scripted radio sound informal and spontaneous and not like a lecture (Scannell and Cardiff, 1991: 166). For some presenters the performance of 'being ordinary' and sounding spontaneous simply reflects their character, but the need to reproduce this consistently for several hours a week or even every day makes this much more of a performance than it might appear.

The ordinariness of talk on radio and the performance of being ordinary is related to another concept developed by Scannell, 'co-presence'. The key to the success of a lot of contemporary radio is the sense communicated by the presenter or DJ that somehow (s)he and the listener exist in the same place at the same time. So when we switch on our radio in the morning and hear 'it's another beautiful day here in downtown Memphis' (or wherever) we are being encouraged to feel a sense of 'being with' that presenter in the same place at the same time. The performance of being ordinary by the presenter adds to that sense of co-presence and shared experience and these are communicated largely (though not entirely) through broadcast talk. This sense of shared participation in everyday life is probably easier to achieve on radio than television because the presenter is not an objectified presence on a screen. A sense of co-presence is much more difficult to experience with the carefully made-up presenters of day-time television addressing us from their studio couch than it is with the disembodied voice of a well-known DJ.

Another related feature of broadcast talk that compliments its ordinariness and adds to that sense of co-presence is its 'liveness'. Up until the middle part of the 20th century almost all radio was live. The listener knew that the words coming from the wireless receiver were being spoken at that very moment in time, usually by someone in a studio in front of a microphone. Although a lot of what we now hear on radio is pre-recorded, the 'rhetoric of liveness' is still dominant in radio (see the entry on **Liveness**). Arguably, one of radio's great strengths, and one of the reasons why it survives in an age apparently dominated by visual media and forms of audio on demand such as the MP3 player or over the Internet, is its insistence on live communication. I say 'insistence' because the word 'live' is continually used by presenters to affirm this essential virtue; 'coming to you live ...', 'right here live on ...', and so on. In broadcast talk the liveness of radio is communicated in the spontaneity and immediacy of the talk. What we hear feels more live partly because the references made by presenters and DJs are to today's events (nationally or locally) but also because the talk contains the 'ums' and 'errs' and pauses of unscripted and spontaneous speech.

If we examine an example of broadcast talk we can see the interplay of these different characteristics of radio. Karen Atkinson and Shaun Moores (2003) have analysed the phone-in programme *Live and Direct*, which was broadcast in the late 1990s on the British national commercial radio station Talk Radio (now called talkSPORT) and presented by Anna Raeburn. As they point out, the title of the programme captured that sense of liveness and immediacy. The programme encouraged callers to discuss personal problems with the well-known presenter in a programme genre typical of the 'therapeutic advice-giving' developed on US radio in the 1970s. Although Raeburn was giving advice she presented herself not as a therapist or expert but as an ordinary person, someone just like the caller, as this extract shows:

> I don't fix anything (1.0) you do (1.0) what we offer on freecall 0500 105839 is the chance to talk (2.0) to check out a range of options (.) to run the decision by somebody who has no vested interest in anything but you (.) telling often the uncomfortable truth as I see it (1.0) and I would just like to remind you at this stage that I'm human too (.) just as fallible just as vulnerable just as bashed about and world-weary as you are (.) so if you want to talk about something and you're worried about it and you feel foolish and silly and small don't bother (.) everyone else feels just as (laughing) foolish just as silly just as small (.) that's the predicament (.) and if you'd like to join us that number once more is freecall 0500 105839. (Atkinson and Moores, 2003: 133 – The numbers in brackets indicate the length of a pause in seconds. (.) indicates a short pause)

The pauses, laughter and direct address all contribute to the liveness and apparent spontaneity of this talk. Anna Raeburn also portrays herself as just an ordinary person ('I'm human too') and in her use of 'we', 'everyone else' and 'join us' she fosters a powerful sense of co-presence with and among her listeners.

Talk on radio is of course extremely varied depending on genre, format, the target audience, the nature of the station or network, the time of day and so on. The presenter or whoever is talking will also influence broadcast talk depending on their cultural background. News, analysis, documentary, live sport, conversation and different types of music radio will all employ variations of talk. Andrew Tolson, for example, describes BBC Five Live, the news and sport network which, as its name suggests, foregrounds liveness (2006: 94). The emphasis on sport appeals to a working-class, male listener and the commentators and presenters speak with a rich variety of accents and dialects unusual for the BBC. In the Saturday post-match phone-in programme 606 all the characteristics of liveness, co-presence and ordinariness are evident as is the undisputed authority of the presenter. Tolson describes the use of 'confrontation talk' on 606 as the caller and host argue about football in a manner that perfectly (and deliberately) mimics two men in a pub.

The extraordinary variety of broadcast talk is captured by Susan Douglas (1999) in her account of American radio and culture. She describes listening to radio in 1978 in New York. On AM the talk radio host, Bob Grant is yelling 'you creep! Get off the phone!' and 'you mealy-mouthed pompous oaf', at callers to his late night show. Meanwhile on National Public Radio over on FM, Joe Frank is reminiscing about the experience of being a child, 'when you're a child, you're so alive to experience. The world dazzles you, especially the world of living beings' (Douglas, 1999: 284). Different though these examples are, in both cases, and in every case of broadcast talk, the words we hear serve to keep the listener tuned in by evoking spontaneity, ordinariness and co-presence.

FURTHER READING

Scannell's (1991) short collection of articles is an obvious starting point. Tolson's (2006) much more recent book on 'media talk' is very interesting and readable while Atkinson and Moores (2003) is a wonderful example of the analysis of radio talk (and much else besides).

Comedy

> **Comedy is a speech radio genre, which includes a wide variety of entertainment programmes. Comedy is also often a feature of the performance of the radio DJ.**

There is something odd about the success and importance of radio comedy. Why is something so inherently visual (think of facial grimaces, silly clothes, slapstick routines) a success on an invisible medium? To take this point further, comedy has been a vital ingredient in radio's development and success but even highly visual forms of comedy, including ventriloquism, have worked well. This question is posed by Crisell, who also comments that we normally listen to radio alone but laughter, the natural response to comedy, is usually a collective act (1994: 164). Some comedy clearly works well on radio; the simply narrated joke for example or the sitcom based on strong and familiar characters and a good script. But comedy can also exploit the invisibility (or 'blindness') of radio; the iconic 1950s British radio comedy, *The Goon Show*, being a good example. For Crisell this is a 'radiogenic' programme, exploiting the lack of visual images in a surreal audio experience (see the entry on **Radiogenic**).

What exactly is radio comedy? The term 'comedy' is used to describe specific genres of radio; the sitcom, the quiz show, the sketch show, all of which have a comic component. But humour, a state of mind or form of communication which is comic or witty, is a feature not just of comedy programmes, it may also be found in a DJ's presentation, sports coverage or even in a light news item. So what characterises humour? At least one feature is the 'transgressive' quality of humour, the stepping over boundaries of normal decency and taste to mock or even ridicule the serious and important aspects of life. The problem is that such transgressions can quite easily offend and take us to 'the perilous terrain that lies between humour and offensiveness' (Lockyer and Pickering, 2005: 3). So although humour is often seen as a good thing, as a therapeutic way of getting things off our chests, it can easily offend and reinforce prejudices, and especially those against minority or disadvantaged groups. In recent years the mounting tensions between the West and Islam have provided plenty of good examples of this. In 2006, cartoons in a Danish magazine making fun of the Prophet Mohammed led to riots in parts of the world. Any discussion of radio comedy needs to acknowledge comedy's potential to offend, and indeed some radio presenters have deliberately strived to do just that.

The histories of radio reveal how central comedy has been in the development of the medium. In the USA there can be few more famous or infamous programmes than *Amos 'n' Andy*, first broadcast in 1928 and featuring two white actors playing the parts of two black 'country bumpkins' who have recently arrived in Chicago. In her discussion of the programme, Hilmes notes that at the time there was almost a complete absence of black performers and producers in 'radio's resolutely white address' (1997: 75). Here is a short extract from an earlier show, *Sam 'n' Henry*:

Sam: Henry, did you ever see a mule as slow as dis one?
Henry: Oh, dis mule is fast enough. We gonna get to de depot alright.
Sam: You know dat Chicago train don't wait for nobody – it just goes on – just stops and goes right on.
Henry: Well, we ain't got but two blocks to go – don't be so patient, don't be so patient.
Sam: I hope they got faster mules dan dis up in Chicago. (Cited in Hilmes, 1997: 87)

This needs little comment. In addition to their ungrammatical and confused use of English, the two main characters are depicted in the most stereotypical fashion. Amos and Andy were variously lazy, stupid, superstitious, manipulative and prone to womanising. This minstrel-inspired early comedy made the black American experience more visible but did so in a patronising and excluding manner.

Today we would find the thought of two white men painting their faces black and pretending to be rather stupid African Americans unacceptable and racist. But we would probably find Mae West's 1937 appearance on *The Chase and Sanborn Hour* (featuring the ventriloquist Edgar Bergen and his dummy Charlie McCarthy) quite acceptable, unlike the audience at the time. West's notorious reputation as a 'loose woman' and her free use of sexual innuendo in the show transgressed sexual taboos of the time and caused widespread offence. The show managed to produce the most vitriolic response because, 'in the space of thirty minutes, during what was to be West's only major radio performance, heterosexual female desire was accorded unprecedented license over the airwaves' (Murray, 2002: 136).

Early British radio comedy, like its American equivalent, also relied on theatrical (or 'music hall') styles and performers. Early BBC comedy was part of the output of Light Entertainment and was characterised by short sketches and stand-up routines. Pre-war comedy provided one of the few places where regional or working-class voices could be heard on the BBC. But working-class comedy was prone to vulgarity and needed to be made safe and inoffensive:

Working-class entertainment was collective, disorderly, immediate – 'vulgar' by definition. Middle-class entertainment was orderly, regulated and calm, and it was this aesthetic that informed the BBC's understanding of listeners' leisure needs ... the problem was to fit entertainment as occasion into an intimate routine, to take pleasures that were essentially live (with the elements of risk and uncertainty) and script them so that nothing untoward happened. (Simon Frith in Barnard, 2000: 111)

The Second World War provided a boost for radio light entertainment, both comedy and popular music, in the absence of cinema and theatre (closed for the duration of the war) and of course before the arrival of television (the pilot London service was also closed during the war years). The BBC saw the need for entertainment to lift the morale of the population and one of the best examples of wartime radio comedy was *It's That Man Again*, (also known as '*ITMA*'): the 'man' referring to Adolph

comedy

Hitler. The show featured 'quick-fire humour and zany characters' and its 310 episodes ran from 1939–1949 (Street, 2006b: 148). As early American radio comedy betrayed a cultural obsession with race so British comedy was so often based on social class. *ITMA* featured gin-soaked colonels and screeching cleaning ladies among its social class stereotypes. In the 1950s *Hancock's Half Hour* featured Tony Hancock, one of radio comedy's most successful performers, colourfully described here by Stephen Wagg: 'The Hancock character is in many ways the model of a dyspeptic, status anxious, petit bourgeois suburbanite stomping grumpily about the reaches of Middle England' (1998: 7).

Although comedy programmes can still be found in radio around the world they have none of the importance of the early shows. Perhaps the dominance of television and film comedy has reasserted the simple fact that this is a genre that seems to work better with visual images. BBC Radio 4 has for some time been a place to find innovative comedy programmes, including sit-coms, sketch and quiz shows, but when these are successful they usually make the switch from radio to television.

If radio comedy, however, is in decline it certainly does not follow that radio has lost its humorous content. In fact humour and irreverence, the transgression of boundaries, is a distinctive feature of the DJ's patter and that of the talk show host. When the DJ was invented in the USA in the late 1940s and early 1950s, their role was partly to create a 'fun' feel to their shows. Music radio, often targeted at youth audiences, includes a discursive space, which expresses youth culture and is invariably comic and entertaining. On BBC Radio 1, the most successful day-time DJs are often the funniest, able to use prepared and ad lib wit to keep the audience listening. The same was true of early examples of talk radio in the USA. The early 'shock jocks' Dom Imus and Howard Stern conveyed an atmosphere of fun in their studios using a cast of characters and the sounds of laughter, rude noises and boisterous disorder. Howard Stern was particularly funny and especially when ridiculing self-important celebrities. Although a great deal of talk radio is serious, an underlying theme of some of the most successful shows is a sense of humour based on irreverence and transgression (see the entries on **Talk Radio** and **DJs and Presenters**).

Listening to live radio today we might think that a good sense of humour is a prerequisite for the successful DJ or presenter. In music, phone-ins, magazines, sport and other forms of live programming the use of wit and repartee are almost universal. Visual gags are, of course, excluded, although they can be described, but the essentially linguistic mode of so much humour, in other words wit, works particularly well on radio. The move towards collective presentation, as in 'zoo' techniques, has greatly enhanced the opportunities to include repartee and comic banter and keep alive the comic radio tradition.

FURTHER READING

The literature on radio comedy is disappointingly thin but for a general introduction see Crisell (1994: 164–85). Hilmes' (1997) discussion of the early years of American radio comedy shows how comedy served to reinforce racial stereotypes. In addition many of the classic British and American comedies are available commercially.

DJs and Presenters

> Radio DJs and presenters provide the spoken and performed link between the programme content and the radio audience.

The music radio DJ (or disc jockey) and the presenter of speech radio are both operating at the interface between the audience and the radio station (Hendy, 2000: 57). Largely through their use of broadcast talk and their persona, DJ/presenters have a key role to play in making radio listening possible and desirable. Their performance is often important in the creation of station identity as well as building and maintaining a regular listening audience. In this entry I am going to look at DJs and presenters jointly because the similarities between the two of them are so great, but there are important differences too.

In her historical account of the rise of the American DJ, Douglas sees this as a phenomenon of the 1950s and concurrent with the introduction of the transistor radio and its resulting popularity with American youth (Douglas, 1999: 229). She cites the example of the influential 'superjock' Wolfman Jack, the persona of the radio businessman Bob Smith. Like other early radio DJs, Wolfman Jack used his magnetic and cool personality to connect with the growing teenage audience. Unlike the pre-war 'emcees', who joked with their studio audiences, the new radio DJs spoke directly to the individual listener, embracing and flattering their youth. A part of the illicit attraction of DJs like Wolfman was their racial pedigree: the origins of rhythm and blues and rock 'n' roll lay in African American music and many DJs used slang from the ghetto to reinforce their cool and non-white credentials.

In both the USA and the UK, the radio DJ has come to do what Douglas described in her account of early DJ talk:

> DJ talk had to be invented and had to serve – and mediate between – very particular cultural and corporate interests. It was a monologue that sounded like a dialogue. The talk had to dramatize and personify the station's identity, and it had to make the audience feel personally included in the show, feel sought out and enfolded into a special, distinct community. (1999: 230)

So the DJ is in effect facing in two different directions; at the corporate boss (or public service broadcaster) but also at the listener. In doing so the DJ is at the centre of music radio and this is physically represented by the layout of the radio studio in which the DJ operates the equipment and presents the show from the desk (Starkey, 2004a: 63).

Most of the literature on DJs, such as it is, tends to focus on their performative use of talk (see the entry on **Broadcast Talk**). So, for example, much has been said about the way the DJ uses direct speech ('you', 'we', 'I') to create an intimacy with the listener and also to conjure a simulated sense of 'co-presence', the sense that the listener has of being with the presenter and also with other members of the audience (Montgomery, 1986: 428). Modern DJs, often using a phone, may talk directly to a named listener who has phoned the show. In this case other listeners find themselves cast as 'overhearers' to a one-to-one conversation. In this talk it is important to recognise that the DJ is always in control, no matter how informal and jokey they may be with their listeners. This is particularly well illustrated by the case of *The Tony Blackburn Show* (1984–1989, BBC Radio London). While creating a carefully crafted and highly complex persona, Blackburn built a discursive space (what I call in a separate entry, a '**radio world**'), which has 'tightly defined boundaries' (Brand and Scannell, 1991: 223).

The modern radio DJ is very much a part of celebrity culture, often vying for celebrity with the music stars whose music they play. The radio DJ as celebrity will foreground their own performance and identity at the expense of the music they play, for example by talking over the beginning and end of songs. They may also appear in a variety of other media; on television, in the press and in magazines. The celebrity status of some DJs is a way of retaining radio audiences in the face of competition from portable music players playing audio on demand. An interesting variation on this theme is the 'music star as radio DJ'. Bob Dylan's experiments as a DJ playing his own choice of music is a good example of another way of maintaining the appeal of the genre.

There is something fundamentally conservative and traditional about music radio and the role of the radio DJ. Very little has changed since the introduction of Top-40 radio in the mid-1950s in which DJs played repeatedly the top 40 hit records in the charts. The speech radio presenter, however, is quite different in the sheer variety of genres for which they are needed. Quiz shows, comedy, news magazines, current affairs, talk radio phone-ins; all require a presenter performing differently in each case. In pre-war British radio the widespread use of news 'announcers' and radio talks meant there was little need for presenters as we know them today. In addition, because almost all speech on the BBC was scripted, the role of the presenter as 'referee' or interviewer was simply unnecessary. An exception was the early, unscripted discussion programme, *Men Talking* (1937) for which a 'chairman' was used to guide (or control) the discussions. It was the introduction of the magazine programme during the Second World War, in programmes such as *The Kitchen Front* mainly designed for women, and also in panel programmes such as *The Brains Trust* that made the presenter or 'chairman' necessary.

In the USA, journalists were increasingly used to 'anchor' radio news and an early and very important example of this is the CBS war-time news sequence *Foreign News Roundup*, presented (or 'anchored') from London by Edward R. Murrow. He brought together the reports of journalists in different European cities as the war unfolded as well as providing his own distinctive war reports.

Gradually the news (or current affairs) magazine became a feature of British radio as well and in particular from the 1960s when the traditional boundary between news and comment in the BBC began to break down. Here is a particularly graphic description of a news presenter from the 1960s:

William Hardcastle, who had been a Washington Correspondent for Reuters after the War and an Editor of the *Daily Mail* ... was a large, beetle-browed, untidy person, cigarette-smoking, hard-drinking and shirt-sleeved, and he brought to *The World at One* some of the urgency and heat of Fleet Street. His breathless delivery mangled the conventions of measured speech that still held sway across most of the Home Service, and prompted a regular flow of complaint by disappointed listeners. (Hendy, 2007: 48)

British speech radio has produced a procession of famous and highly accomplished presenters who, often presenting the same programme over a long period of time, have come to be identified with, or even to be the identity of, the programmes they present. On commercial radio, Brian Hayes presented a morning phone-in sequence from the mid-1970s to 1990; BBC Radio 4's *Woman's Hour* has been presented by Jenni Murray since 1985 and on the flagship radio current affairs programme, *Today*, John Humphrys has been intimidating politicians for 20 years.

The emergence of **talk radio** in the USA in the early 1970s produced one of the most extreme forms of speech presenter and importantly one that combined characteristics of both the radio DJ and the speech presenter. The shock jock used a variety of sexual references and obscenities, often combined with right-wing or libertarian political views, to literally shock their listeners and entertain them at the same time. The persona of the shock jock was epitomised by Howard Stern:

> Stern's on-air persona was that of the class trouble-maker – and often the bully – in seventh grade, the guy who made fart noises during study hall and tried to snap girls' bra straps in the cafeteria. He was obsessed with sex and was also relentlessly self-absorbed. One of the adjectives most frequently used to describe him was *pubescent*. (Douglas, 1999: 304)

Another similarity between shock jocks and DJs is in the boundary maintenance they exercise over their **radio world**. Although an impression of libertarian anarchy was conveyed on their shows this was never at the expense of tight control over what listeners could say on air. Indeed an abusive control over callers was a feature of talk radio as far back as the 1960s when the Los Angeles presenter Joe Pyne told those with whom he disagreed to 'go gargle with razor blades'. Similarly, the phone-in presenter, Brian Hayes, on the London commercial station LBC, efficiently and briskly processed callers in order to extract whatever newsworthy comment they had to make. The appearance of an equal and friendly relationship between presenter and caller was maintained but the presenter is always in charge and callers are simply 'processed' within the strict routines of the show (Hutchby, 1991: 130).

There are few notable examples of presenters who worked successfully as both DJs and speech presenters but one such broadcaster was the veteran DJ John Peel. From the 1960s and the era of pirate radio in the UK and the launch of BBC Radio 1, Peel was the main champion of music beyond the limits of the charts. He discovered and promoted the most innovative British music, including punk, and as a DJ typified the knowledgeable guide introducing listeners to new music, which they would otherwise never have heard. Towards the end of his life, Peel also started to introduce speech radio and was particularly successful on the BBC Radio 4 Saturday morning magazine *Home Truths* (1998–2006). Once again, the creation of a radio persona lay at the heart of Peel's success. He presented himself as a family man, a rather bewildered character confronted by the fads, gadgets and mores of the modern world. He made a unique 'radio world' in which listeners were encouraged to contribute their own crafted writings which mirrored his own eccentricities. Over the years that he presented the programme he became an ironic and self-deprecating sceptic, celebrating these same qualities in his listeners (Chignell and Devlin, 2007).

So long as speech radio survives, and in particular in news and comment, and entertaining factual programming, it is surely true that radio presenters will continue to personify the programmes they present, help the listener make sense of the different voices featured and keep the unruly callers in order. The fate of the radio DJ is far less certain. The death of the radio DJ is a popular theme with the rise of 'voice tracking' and 'cyber jocking', the deadening influence of ultra-niche assembly line radio and the ever-present threat of audio on demand MP3 players. But as Keith and Sterling point out, the story of the radio DJ may have gone full circle (2004: 473). The amateurs of web radio or podcasting may reclaim radio once again from the stars and personalities of presentation. Once again the voice that presents the music, like the nameless announcers of the 1920s and 1930s, will be unknown.

FURTHER READING

There is some very interesting and insightful work on the performance of the radio DJ but very little indeed on the speech presenter. Douglas (1999: 219–56) discusses the rise of the DJ in the USA in the 1950s and 1960s. Montgomery's (1986) early article on the DJ is an important and influential contribution as is Brand and Scannell (1991) on Tony Blackburn. John Peel's presentation of the speech programme *Home Truths* is one of the few discussions of speech radio presentation (Chignell and Devlin, 2007).

Documentaries and Features

> *Radio documentaries and features are both factual radio genres. Documentaries share many of the characteristics of the television documentary but features are often more creative incorporating a wider variety of speech and music.*

Radio documentaries and features are really two different genres but they are in most respects so similar it makes sense to consider them in one entry. Radio documentaries, like their television counterpart, are factual accounts of 'reality' often based on interviews, observation and actuality. The term radio 'feature' can be traced back to the pre-war BBC and the Features Department. An early features producer in the BBC, Laurence Gilliam, wrote that the term 'radio feature' had come to signify 'a wide range of programme items, usually factual and documentary, presented by a variety of techniques, but mostly making use of dramatisation and edited actuality' (1950: 9). This strange radio hybrid, unique to radio and like nothing to be found on television, has existed both in Britain and in the USA.

Radio documentaries continue to survive, just, on public service radio around the world and are often remarkably similar to television documentaries. It is sometimes not easy, however, to distinguish between radio documentaries and current affairs. The latter, however, is far more journalistic and prioritises factual information, presented in a well-structured and balanced way. The radio documentary is more likely to exploit the possibilities of sound, often in the representation of an aspect of everyday life. Crisell (1994) has controversially accused radio of being a 'blind medium' (see entry on **Blindness**) but the ambiguity of the messages of radio that he describes can be used to advantage in the documentary. Hendy argues that radio documentary, unconcerned by the visual priorities of television, can take seemingly bland, everyday phenomena and create something 'rich in meanings' (2004: 173). He takes the example of a programme about collecting (for example collecting beer mats, records or insects) which can quickly take on wider significance to become a programme 'about passion, or obsession, or loneliness, or sociability, or indeed all of these and more' (2004: 174).

The radio feature, almost extinct now, is a particularly intriguing radio phenomenon. It is unusual in radio output because it is so radio specific: there is simply no equivalent on any other media of its eclectic mix of sound. Features exploit the sonic qualities and diversity of radio; speech (spontaneous and scripted including prose and poetry), music and varieties of other sound (both artificial and actuality) are all available to the features producer. This diversity and the attempt to create a 'built' or crafted programme were originally made possible by the introduction of sound recording in the 1930s. One important producer of pre-war UK features was Olive Shapley who used one of the seven-ton, 27-foot long BBC recording vans to go out and record the voices of homeless people, shoppers, barge people working on the canals, long-distance lorry drivers and people in an all-night café (Scannell and Cardiff, 1991: 345). Back in the studio Shapley used the newly invented Dramatic Control Panel, which enabled her to combine recorded sound with a variety of studio presentation, music and commentary.

You would be right to see a political dimension to Shapley's work, and the potential of radio features to make an explicitly political statement was not lost on either side of the Atlantic. In the USA, from the late 1930s to the late 1940s, a cultural front emerged that expressed the various 'progressive' or radical political movements of the time, including anti-fascism, trade unionism and challenges to segregation and other left-wing causes (Smith, 2002: 210). Radio offered an opportunity to express these political views and also to challenge the white, middle-class bias of radio's imagined audience. In a manner remarkably similar to the British features tradition there was an attempt to retell history and to recover the voices and experiences of ordinary working-class people so long ignored.

The great US radio dramatist and features maker Norman Corwin, made the 'dramatised documentary' *They Fly Through the Air with the Greatest of Ease* (1939) which condemned the actions of airmen who bombed and strafed innocent people in war. At the beginning of the Second World War in Europe, the USA was neutral but even so this was a radical programme. Corwin's most famous 'dramatised documentary', *We Hold These Truths* was broadcast in 1941, just one week after the attack on Pearl Harbour. It was made to mark the 150th anniversary of the Bill of Rights and was broadcast on all networks simultaneously to an audience of 60 million. It praised the ordinary citizen and in particular the soldier-citizen. After the war, Corwin travelled to Europe to make an ambitious 13-part series on the 'status of mankind' (evidence of the extraordinary ambition of radio at the time!):

> In one programme he interviewed a widowed Italian woman and observed: 'This voice and the echo of guns only lately stilled, and the silence of the cemeteries … and the begging of alms, and the whimper of hungry children; this voice, and the mute rubble of wasted towns and cities – these were the sounds of need: need for the hope and for the reality of a united world'. (Keith, 2004: 407)

This quotation is revealing because it shows both Corwin's political romanticism (a trait also evident in later UK features) and also his poetic use of words to evoke a response in his listeners.

In post-war Britain the arrival of the magnetic tape recorder in the early 1950s made the imaginative gathering of speech and actuality possible, and this was fully exploited in the remarkable work of Charles Parker, whose eight *Radio Ballads* (1958–1963) combined the speech of working-class people with folk song and actuality. Parker was influenced by both the folk song and oral history traditions of the time and *The Ballad of John Axon* (1958) was a typical example telling the story of a railwayman killed in an accident trying to halt a runaway train. Parker celebrated the speech of ordinary people, vernacular English as opposed to 'BBC English' and the powerful combination of the vernacular with folk music was an important development in this politicised form of radio. Writing about *John Axon*, Street claims that ' its blending of actuality, natural speech and music narrative into a continuous montage changed the thinking about how features were made' (2004: 189).

Aficionados of radio continue to listen to and value Parker's radio features but even at the time they were seen as part of a dated radio tradition, not in tune with the more audience-friendly and populist mood of the 1960s. Despite the closure of the BBC's Features Department in the early 1960s the genre managed to live on and most dramatically in the epic 26-part series *The Long March of Everyman* (1971–1972). That this was undoubtedly a part of the great tradition of radio features associated with Corwin and Parker was reinforced by Parker's own involvement as 'Producer for the Voices of the People'. Like those who went before him, the producer of *The Long March* had extraordinary ambitions for his feature. He wanted to create the 'Great music of audio', a new art form no less which would once again dramatise the voices of ordinary people down the centuries and would consist of the:

> Ordinary talk of ordinary people; poetry; prose fiction; folk-song; historical documents; natural sound; radiophonic sound; the reflection and analysis of the learned; drama; the expertise of actors, instrumentalists, singers; radiophonically treated speech. All these things can be orchestrated to create a 'new sound' which is something more than all its components taken separately. (Mason, M. in Hendy, 2007: 64)

As David Hendy points out in his history of BBC Radio 4, *The Long March* was certainly epic in scale with contributions from some of the UK's leading historians and was a 'production effort of Herculean proportions' (2007: 65). It did, however, get a very mixed reaction from reviewers who sympathised with the modern radio listener, often listening on a cheap transistor radio in a busy house while doing something else. The days of the classic radio feature seemed to be numbered in a world where radio had fundamentally changed to be the soundtrack of people's lives rather than some sort of sonic theatrical performance.

It would be wrong to see the radio documentary , or even the radio feature, as of only historical interest. I would suggest two reasons why the genre survives, if not as a grandiose political statement in the spirit of Corwin and Parker. First, the radio producer equipped with relatively cheap and unobtrusive sound recording technology can easily record people talking and going about their business without too much intrusion and distortion. As a record of everyday life and of 'ordinary people' it is hard to beat the cheaply made radio documentary aimed, as it often is, at the small but discerning audience and beyond the intimidating glare of television. Second, the radio documentary seems to have found an important place in the output of UK music radio. BBC Radio 2, for example, often broadcasts specialist music documentaries (on the birth of country music, how a songwriter gets inspiration, the early career of a famous performer), which have proved to be particularly popular with an audience of music fans. In the music documentary, archived performance and recordings can be combined with interviews with musicians and fans to greatly enrich the listeners' knowledge and pleasure.

This is a growing area of interest within radio studies and a useful starting point is Hendy (2004). The same writer's history of BBC Radio 4 is also full of references to BBC features and documentaries (Hendy, 2007). Keith (2004) provides a useful introduction to the work of Norman Corwin, while Street (2004) looks at the continuing relevance of Charles Parker.

Drama

> **Drama is a radio genre which features the radio play. Radio drama includes complete 'one off' plays and longer running serials.**

Radio drama is perhaps a contradiction. How is it possible in such a visual age for 'invisible' drama, drama without faces or scenery, to exist? The truth is that, with a few notable and even distinguished exceptions, it has, like radio comedy and radio soaps, partly disappeared. But this is not the complete story. Radio drama has some vociferous advocates, including many of those radio scholars who have helped create a distinct 'radio studies' within the study of the mass media. In addition there is evidence in the recent developments in 'new media' (including both radio and audio) that there is a future for this genre. The structure of this entry is slightly different from some of the others; it starts with a brief history of radio drama and then considers the arguments of what might be called the 'sceptics' and the 'advocates'. It might be useful to read this in conjunction with the entry on radio **Soaps and Serials**.

The introduction and survival of radio drama in the USA and the UK is often connected to a desire to show evidence of 'quality' in broadcasting. The US radio networks in the 1920s and 1930s, for example, were keen to show the cultural calibre of their output and used single dramas for that purpose. The commercial nature of US radio often led to conflict between broadcasters, listeners and members of Congress over the quality of radio output. Network broadcasting was made possible only by commitment to

key concepts in radio studies

the sort of public service and cultural content associated with the BBC: 'The National Broadcasting Company in its opening declaration promised the same kind of promotion of the culturally desirable and exclusion of the culturally suspect that systems such as the BBC made overtly, behind a façade of consumer choice' (Hilmes, 1997: 10). What form did this early, 'quality' radio drama take? A popular approach was to recreate Broadway stage plays for radio. From 1929, NBC's *The First Nighter* regularly recreated Broadway hits. This approach was then followed by *The Lux Radio Theatre* but the obvious limitations of this approach, its reliance on a finite supply of plays written not for radio but for the stage, led to the production team moving to Hollywood. Here plays were presented by the famous film director Cecil B. DeMille and performed by Hollywood stars. Towards the end of the 1930s the networks were under renewed criticism arising from concerns about monopoly, cross-media ownership and the potentially harmful effects of radio on its audience. The networks responded to the criticism in two main ways. Increased airtime was offered to the government and in particular to President Roosevelt who used it to broadcast his famous 'Fireside Chats'. Another response to the criticism was found once again in high profile radio drama. The theatre director Orson Welles was 'the boy genius of the New York stage' (Hilmes, 1997: 218). In 1938, his Mercury Theatre performed as *The Mercury Theatre of the Air* and began with nine adaptations of the 'classics' of literature; *Treasure Island, Dracula, A Tale of Two Cities* and, most famously, *The War of the Worlds* were all adapted for radio as part of the networks' strategy of stressing the quality of their output.

In Britain, post-war radio drama was particularly interesting. The reorganisation of the BBC radio networks after the war led to the creation of the explicitly high cultural Third Programme (one of three 'networks' in BBC radio). With its commitment to the arts and innovation this became a hothouse of avant-garde drama. As television became increasingly popular and populist 'radio at its most esoteric became freer to innovate and explore' (Street, 2002: 88). The Third Programme in this period broadcast some of the most famous of all radio plays, specifically written to exploit the medium of radio; including Dylan Thomas's *Under Milk Wood* (1954) and Samuel Beckett's *All That Fall* (1957).

In his history of BBC Radio 4, Hendy discusses at some length the state of BBC radio drama in the 1970s and early 1980s, which by that time was largely confined to BBC Radio 4. If drama survived on radio, he suggests, it was, it seemed, merely by accident, or through a dutiful signal from the BBC of its continuing faith in the creative dimensions of the medium: an act of tokenism that could be – and probably would be – extinguished at any moment. In the television age it appeared to be living beyond its allotted time (Hendy, 2007). In fact radio drama continued to survive at the BBC and at that time had about 30 drama producers in what was the centre of radio drama production in the English-speaking world. But Radio 4 had then, and still has, a famously conservative, middle-class audience with very precise ideas about what they did or did not like. Much of the output was 'safe', most notably the endless reworking of the 'canon' of English literature; Dickens, Austen, Trollope and so on. The problem was that Radio 4's drama output seemed to have woven about itself an aura of cloying, suburban predictability. This is not to say that there was no innovation and one of the most important developments was the use of more 'filmic' approaches to drama production including the use of location recording: an early example of this was *Why I Did It* (1976), recorded on a staircase at Broadcasting House and in the street outside. This combination of an overall conformity with occasional moments of innovation and brilliance is also noted by Peter Lewis (2004). He comments on the fact that in the mid-1980s there were 10,000 or more drama scripts submitted to the BBC each year. This level of supply tended to increase conformity as writers competed to achieve an acceptable style and content. At the same time the use of location recording had the potential to create atmospheric and successful drama. This pattern on BBC radio of a very large output of rather banal dramas combined with some occasional moments of brilliance has continued to this day.

Despite the global decline of radio drama in the face of the remorseless rise of music formats and other populist output, it still has its supporters. For some commentators there is something rather extraordinary and magical about radio's ability to set a scene, draw a character and tell a story. Shingler and Wieringa claim that there are two main areas of radio drama's artistic strength, '(i) its spatial and temporal flexibility, and (ii) its access to the inner recesses of the mind; both of which are the direct result of being invisible' (1998: 88). They argue that radio's invisibility is an asset that some drama producers embrace and exploit. At a mundane level the absence of lighting, cameras, make-up, scenery and a host of actors all make radio drama relatively cheap – hence the sheer quantity of drama on BBC Radio 4 but also the freedom to innovate at times. The ability to move rapidly from scene to scene and to move about in time is another advantage. In addition, the fact that radio plays are in effect staged 'inside our heads' not on a set or stage produces an intimate quality as we create the *mise-en-scene* (scenery, costumes, actors' movements and so on) for ourselves. Even more enthusiastic about radio drama is Crook, who savages the accusation that radio is 'blind' (see the entry on **Blindness**), asserting that although there are no visual images '... it cannot be said that the ear cannot see. Blind people see' (1999: 7). He explains this by referring to the power of the brain to visualise and imagine a drama communicated by sound. Crook also points out that in the cinema hearing is as important as seeing:

> Which comes first in the experience of film consumption by the audience? Seeing or hearing? If dramatic development and introduction and development of character are communication through sound then their artistic importance in film should be elevated and consolidated to a degree unacknowledged by most film studies scholars. (1999: 25)

For Crook, and other advocates of radio drama, the flexibility of the medium, combined with its ability to create dramas inside our heads, is evidence that it has a future. To dismiss radio drama as an archaic left-over from the days when radio was the dominant medium is to seriously undervalue the importance of sound and hearing. The dominance of the visual in contemporary culture should not lead us to ignore the importance and potential of purely aural drama (that is to say, drama received by the ear).

It would be wrong to deny the existence of radio drama outside US and UK public service radio. In Kenya, for example, the state-owned radio station, KBC, has broadcast up to 54 plays a year on *Radio Theatre* (see the entry on **Development**). In *Not Now* a young girl escapes becoming the fourth wife of an old man. The story is told as a dramatic monologue delivered by the girl, now a woman looking back on her life. In her discussion of the play, and Kenyan radio drama more generally, Dina Ligaga shows how everyday life (the 'quotidian') and language can be enacted through 30-minute plays. These not only reflect the lives of people, especially in the use of local languages and with reference to familiar spaces, they also communicate 'moral lessons' in tune with the government's development agenda. In the case of *Not Now* the message is an unambiguous disapproval of forced marriage.

Radio undoubtedly has the power to produce extremely high quality drama and there are many important examples of the genre. The question remains, however, if it can survive in the modern radio environment. In Britain there is plenty of drama on the air but it is almost entirely

drama

29

restricted to its BBC Radio 4 ghetto. The demographic of the Radio 4 audience, with an average age of over 50, suggests that drama is popular with an audience who may have grown up listening to radio at a time when mainstream children's radio still existed. There is evidence, however, that various forms of audio-on-demand may come to the assistance of this beleaguered genre. Unlike a great deal of other radio output, drama does not necessarily benefit from being live. If the right kind of dramatic material could be produced to suit the Internet or MP3 player then this may provide a way forward. The continued existence and popularity of the audio book suggests that there is a market for extended fictional audio narratives.

FURTHER READING

A very useful introduction to radio drama is Shingler and Wieringa (1998: 73–93). For some historical background, Hilmes (1997: 218–29) details the very important pre-war career of Orson Welles. There are also important sections on BBC radio drama in Hendy (2007). One of the most important discussions of British radio drama is by Crook (1999).

Magazines

> *A style of speech radio programme in which the content is divided up into short items or features.*

The radio magazine is the audio equivalent of the print magazine and has many of the advantages of the latter in terms of its flexibility and relatively undemanding qualities. In Britain, the magazine has become a widely used format in the speech network BBC Radio 4, where it is used for both general magazines, which range over a wide variety of topics, and more specialist magazines which appeal to a smaller target audience. The radio magazine was a largely American invention of the 1920s which, after the war, began to spread to British radio and is now the preferred format for the regular factual output on Radio 4.

Historically, the radio magazine is associated with a female and domestic audience. In the 1920s in the USA, day-time programmes targeted at women were extremely popular and populist to the point of being tabloid. The colourful magazine publisher Bernarr Macfadden produced titles like *New York Graphic, Physical Culture* and *True Romances*. Unsurprisingly he saw the potential in the new medium of radio for an extension to his magazine empire. In 1927, *True Story Hour* appeared on CBS to be followed by other magazines including *True Detective Mysteries* and *True Romances*. The first of these radio magazines was clearly aimed at women, 'originally, *True Story* may have provided the closest thing to an untrammelled venue for young urban women's voices in the public media' (Hilmes, 1997: 100). It was largely based on stories sent in by listeners and which included 'I killed my child', 'I want you', 'How can I face myself' and 'I let him cheapen me'. The themes were of particular concern to women at the time and, controversially, returned repeatedly to the subject of sex. Few of the Macfadden radio magazines survived into the 1930s but there were other, tamer women's magazines providing a 'home service' of domestic advice for the 'housewife'. *The Women's Magazine of the Air* was launched on NBC in 1928 and by 1932 there were over 20 'home service' magazines. The most successful women's magazine was Mary Margaret McBride's daily day-time show which ran for over 20 years into the 1950s and made McBride a huge radio celebrity. When the war effort called for paper for recycling, McBride supplied three million letters, which her adoring listeners had written to her (Hilmes, 1997: 278). An important feature of her success was her ability to present using unscripted speech and to combine a wide variety of items, both serious news and current affairs, with celebrity interviews and other lighter fare.

Meanwhile, on the BBC, the magazine format first appeared in the 1930s with programmes such as *In Town Tonight* and *The World Goes By*. These all featured the 'human interest approach' in which ordinary people spoke about the sometimes humorous aspects of their daily lives. The BBC North Region's folksy *Owt Abaht Owt* (loosely translated as 'anything about anything') might offer a table of contents containing 'an aerial flood-shooter, a harmonizing boy's club, a well-known Northern itinerant bagger of gags, an inveterate drummer, a master of mistletoe and a pantomime star' (Scannell and Cardiff, 1991: 175). During the Second World War, the radio magazine was a particularly successful format for advising women about how to prepare food during a time of considerable scarcity and food rationing. From 1940, *The Kitchen Front* consisted mainly of informative talks to start with but gradually became a more general talks magazine with celebrity visitors and even a 'comedy housewife' (Nicholas, 1996: 78).

The BBC's most successful magazine targeted explicitly at women is *Woman's Hour* (1946–present). In all of that time the programme has addressed 'women's concerns' (more and more broadly defined) and retained a format that includes a dominant female presenter (although the first presenter was, remarkably, a man), interviews and other short feature items, discussions and a drama serial.

The success and ubiquitous nature of the radio magazine on UK speech radio reflects the realisation, almost 40 years ago, that the listener was no longer prepared to listen to complete speech programmes and preferred to dip in and out of something more fragmented. If we take the example of current affairs, there is clearly a place on public service speech radio for in-depth, single subject investigations of political and social issues (see the separate entry on **Current Affairs**). On BBC Radio 4, however, the daily news magazine *Today* has all but replaced the more weighty and longer form investigation with a fast-paced, itemised treatment of the major news stories. Short, often hard hitting, interviews with politicians and others in the news are combined with equally brief on the spot reports by BBC correspondents in 'two-way' interviews with the anchor presenters. There can be no doubt that this approach fits the way radio is listened to in the morning while seeming to remain a serious and comprehensive treatment of news stories.

In his history of BBC Radio 4, Hendy describes the way that the magazine was introduced across the schedule during the early 1970s. The arts programme *Kaleidoscope* (1973–1997) was a daily arts magazine that replaced the more serious and taxing talks programmes such as *The Critics*. For some of the BBC's own critics this was evidence of the dumbing down and trivialisation of radio (Hendy, 2007: 81). Furthermore, remembering the origins of the radio magazine, these same critics saw the introduction of the format as evidence of the Americanisation of British culture, at the time one of the worst slurs that could be used against the BBC. The fact that such criticisms are no longer heard and sound implausible today is probably a testament to the ability of the radio magazine to deal with both light and entertaining items as well as much more serious material.

FURTHER READING

There is some important historical writing on the phenomenon of the radio magazine. Hilmes (1997: 97–130) discusses the pre-war American magazine and there is an excellent account of British war-time radio magazines in Nicholas (1996). Hendy (2007) has a full discussion of the 'magazinisation' of BBC Radio 4.

Music

Music is one of the codes of radio and a universally important content of radio programming.

Imagine two people listening to the same piece of music. One of them has an MP3 player (or something similar) and chose this record from among many others. The other person is listening to the local radio station, which is playing this record at the same time. The same music at the same time but one is radio and the other is not. The concept of music radio, the reason for its existence, lies in the fact that the radio experience is somehow different and indeed is in some ways better than just listening to pre-recorded music. There seem to be four major features of music radio that distinguish it. First, the music played has been chosen by someone else and not by the listener; second, most music radio is live and gives the listener a sense of co-presence with others; third, the music played is accompanied by the words of the DJ who frames the music and adds meaning or significance to it and, finally, radio stations and their audiences have a constructed identity (often around notions of youth) which the experience of listening reinforces.

The words 'music' and 'radio' have been endlessly combined in the existing literature on radio. This is usually in the form of 'music radio' as opposed to what might be called 'radio music'; the first referring to radio programming, which mainly consists of recorded 'popular music', and the latter meaning the composed sound that is used to enhance radio presentation (in the form of music beds, station 'idents', signature tunes and so on). The main interest here is to write about music radio itself and to try to answer some basic questions. What is music radio and why is it like it is? Why is music radio so dominant in radio programming around the world? What changes seem to be happening to music radio as a result of new technology?

In most parts of the world, music radio is the dominant format and far exceeds radio based on speech programming. In the UK, for example, all local commercial FM radio is music radio and almost all of the stations feature contemporary hits and are targeted at a young audience. On BBC network radio, transmitted to the whole of the UK, Radios 1, 2 and 3 are

music

all music networks and BBC local radio includes a combination of speech and music for its 50-plus target audience. In the USA, with the exception of talk radio and National Public Radio, music radio is dominant. So how have we arrived at a situation where music radio is so ubiquitous? In their discussion of the 'redefinition' of American radio after the Second World War, Rothenbuhler and McCourt (2002) describe the transition from network-dominated mixed programming which existed up to the end of the war, to the situation in the 1960s when most stations were playing chart music for a largely teenage audience. The growth of music radio post-war can be explained by the arrival of television and the crisis this created for radio. The huge success of television forced the radio industry to turn to cheaper ways of reaching the audience and also a search for new audiences. Initially helped by the advent of the transistor radio in 1953, there was a growth in local programming with local DJs playing recorded music (see the entry on **Reception**). Rothenbuhler and McCourt illustrate this by referring to the development of radio for black communities, by 1955 there were over 600 such stations in 39 states. Although 'minority radio', as it was called, often served to reinforce racial stereotypes it also played rhythm and blues and made this music, so important in the evolution of rock and pop, available to white audiences for the first time. In the 1960s in the USA music radio had become increasingly uniform as its commercial potential was fully realised. The emergence of rock and roll and with it a youth culture influenced by iconic figures such as Elvis Presley and James Dean, was intimately connected to the development of Top-40 radio, playing hit records from playlists to a teenage audience with disposable income.

The relentless commercial pressure exerted on radio since the evolution of music radio in the USA in the 1960s has led to the growth of music formats. The intensity of competition between stations has produced increasingly refined music choices to target the audience in new and more exact ways. As Hendy puts it, 'a radio station's decision to play a particular genre of music means it is also choosing a particular audience' (2000: 169). So the music we hear will reflect the station format, be it contemporary hits radio, album orientated rock or contemporary country, and at the same time detailed playlists and careful scheduling all conspire to maximise the audience and keep it listening. In his analysis of a breakfast show, Garner shows how music is carefully chosen to capture the precise mood of the audience at any particular time. As he puts it so memorably, the 'real text' of the breakfast programme is not the music or the lyric but 'the clock on the studio wall' (cited in Hendy, 2000: 174).

How can we explain the dominance of music radio? Or to put it differently, why is there such a natural fit between music and radio? To answer this question it is worth exploring the fundamental nature of music on radio and how it differs from speech. In his application of semiology, the study of signs, to radio, Crisell refers to speech as radio's 'primary code' (1994: 42): see the entry on **Codes** for evidence of this. In his discussion of radio's 'raw material', of the noises and silence we hear over time, he suggests that it is the power of speech to convey meaning that makes it so important. This of course contrasts with film and television in which visual images can be the dominant code. As Crisell acknowledges, music is much harder to examine in semiotic terms because, unlike words and pictures, it appears not to signify anything. It exists on radio as an object of pleasure, which we can assimilate to our own mood as we wish. There is a sense in which listening to music is much easier than listening to speech which requires our effort to interpret its meaning. Music is not handicapped by the invisibility of radio and this is one of the reasons for the dominance of music radio. Music is highly '**radiogenic**' and the partnership between music and radio as been phenomenally successful, 'a partnership which has been crucial to the formation of modern popular culture' (Crisell 1994: 42). But music radio is not just music, it is the framing of music by speech which is the key to its success. See the entry on **DJs and Presenters** for some ideas about how the radio DJ takes the raw material of music and creates a much more meaningful radio experience.

A further aspect of the success and dominance of music radio lies in its ability to reflect and reinforce our sense of identity, as Hendy says, 'if it is true that through radio we *hear what we are*, it is also true that to some extent we *are what we hear*' (2000: 214, original emphasis). The power of the mass media generally to aid the construction of identity is an axiom of media studies. Susan Douglas, for example, provides a particularly vivid account of young women in the USA in the 1960s listening to pop music and finding in it the resource to find themselves:

> The most important thing about this music, the reason it spoke to us so powerfully, was that it gave voice to all the warring selves inside us struggling, blindly and with a crushing sense of insecurity, to forge something resembling a coherent identity. (1994: 87)

Music radio not only reinforces gender and age identities but also national identities. In his discussion of radio in the apartheid era in South

Africa, Hendy describes the way radio was targeted at 'tribal groups' in a deliberate attempt to reinforce ethnic divisions within the black African population. So Radio Bantu played traditional tribal music to emphasise the separate identities of Zulus, Xhosas and so on (Hendy, 2000).

Music radio has the potential to succeed and attract large audiences, especially of young people for whom the music played expresses and helps structure their identity. But this is to be very optimistic and to fail to acknowledge the crushing uniformity of much music radio, driven into the banal repetition of the same commercial product by the highly competitive nature of the radio industry. As both Berland and Douglas have so vividly described, radio has become dominated by a certain type of formatted, uniform, centralised radio which has largely eliminated the nuances of the local and the community (Hendy, 2000: 4). They and many others would treasure those moments in the history of music radio when it has been possible for an original DJ to play not just chart music and engage a local or national audience in an exciting and imaginative way. In British radio one of the best examples of that originality was John Peel who in his long career at BBC Radio 1 played an eclectic range of recorded music and also had live music sessions performed by frequently unknown performers. Some of the greats of contemporary pop including Hendrix and Bowie were largely unknown before they performed live on a Peel show (Garner, 1993).

New technology offers opportunities for music radio and at the same time presents some serious challenges. The ability to download thousands of records and play them back on a tiny portable player seriously challenges the value of traditional music radio. The solution for radio stations has broadly been to reinforce some of the features that make music radio different, the distinct characteristics mentioned at the start of this entry. Specialist music shows, often playing outside peak time, try to introduce listeners to music that they would not otherwise have heard of. In the UK, BBC Radio 1's evening and night-time output is designed to introduce new music and uses specialist presenters. DJs are critical to the success of music radio and the 'celebrity DJ' can draw the listener in and keep them listening; as Crisell puts it so memorably, by acting as a 'broker' between the glamorous world of pop music and 'the mundane concerns of his listeners' (1994: 69). Music radio can also enhance its sense of **'liveness'** and hence the feeling of co-presence by maximising audience interaction. The widespread use of phone-ins, text messaging, competitions and direct references to listeners by name all enhances this feature.

FURTHER READING

Most of the introductions to the study of radio provide interesting analyses of music radio (Crisell, 1994 and Hendy, 2000 are both particularly good). For some historical context, Douglas (1999: 219–56) charts the emergence of pop music radio in the USA. Wall's (T., 2004) discussion of Internet music radio is also a helpful starting point.

Phone-ins

> *The radio phone-in (or 'call in') is a production technique that incorporates listeners' calls into the content of the programme.*

The radio phone-in is a universally popular programming device and has become one of the most important ways of filling the 24-hour radio schedule. The technologies of the phone ('telephony') and radio ('wireless telegraphy') are intimately connected, but the telephone had a head start and in Britain was a fully developed wired network by the time wireless telegraphy was in its experimental stage before the First World War. Before radio broadcasting became established in the 1920s there were various experiments in which concerts and plays were sent down telephone lines. After 1922, however, radio and the telephone went their separate ways until the invention of the radio 'phone-in', 'the term was coined in the United States in 1968 and was first heard as a phrase in the United Kingdom in 1971' (Street, 2006b: 204). More recently, the invention of the mobile or cell phone and the possibility of listening to radio via mobile phones has brought the two technologies back together again in the increasingly convergent communications media.

The first British radio phone-in was on BBC Radio Nottingham in 1968 and, because of the relative cheapness of phone-ins, it became widely used throughout BBC and commercial local radio in the 1970s. On the national BBC networks, the phone-in is still a rarity on Radio 4 but used extensively on the news/sport format of Radio 5 Live. In the USA, 'call-ins' are an established feature of much music programming but they are particularly important in talk radio. Jerry Williams, show *What's On Your Mind?* on a station in Camden, New Jersey in the 1950s may have been the first to take listeners' calls. The talk radio format was born and the distinctive combination of opinionated presenter and callers, many of whom were there to be insulted, became one of the most popular, and politically influential, US formats.

In his discussion of the radio phone-in, Crisell distinguishes between three main types. The 'Expressive' call allows the caller to express their views, often contrary to the consensus; this is particularly important in the case of minority, excluded social groups or where the opinions are themselves minority views. The 'Exhibitionist' call is, as its name implies, an opportunity to project a personality, for someone to exhibit themselves, and the 'Confessional' call seeks advice and uses the relative anonymity of radio to get therapeutic help (Crisell, 1994: 119). He goes on to describe the complexity of an exchange that on one level appears like a private conversation even though in reality it is highly public. 'Thus the phone-in is capable of unique effects within radio, for it is a half-private, half-public medium in which one element of the audience becomes part of the performance and involved in a complex and unusual relationship with the other half' (1994: 197). The appeal of the phone-in is thus partly the pleasure of 'listening in' to an apparently private conversation, what Crisell calls 'aural voyeurism', but also having the potential for phoning ourselves even if we do not. This is, as Shingler and Wieringa put it, 'participation and reciprocation, at best, by proxy' (1998: 114).

A good example of a radio DJ using the phone-in is Chris Evans on BBC Radio in the early 1990s. Evans was something of a celebrity DJ, known in the tabloid press for his late night antics. He pioneered the use of the Zoo format (working with a number of regular contributors in the studio) and was known for a laddish, funny and rather insulting approach to callers. Evans used calls as a way of creating and affirming the community of his listeners and their unique identity, as well as his own kudos as the clever, witty radio celebrity. For listeners, the chance of phoning in meant they could share, if only for a moment, that glamorous world:

> It is, however, a world where anyone can enter the media and, like Amanda [a caller], have their fifteen seconds of fame. It is a world where ordinary people interact with media personnel, and, by extension, the mediated community of the mini-celebrity which they inhabit. (Tolson, 2006: 129)

A very different example is the case of the Anna Raeburn's show *Live and Direct* on the UK station Talk Radio (now called talkSPORT) in the

1990s. This is an example of the 'confessional phone-in' or therapy radio. What is interesting about it is the considerable skill of the presenter and her ability to employ a wide repertoire of reactions to the often very emotional comments of her listeners. She used humour, she 'broadened the relevance' of the caller's problems, sometimes she diffused their despair, she identified with callers or chose not to, sometimes she spoke to the caller but at others addressed them and the audience (Atkinson and Moores, 2003). Both Evans and Raeburn were extremely skilled broadcasters who were able to use a range of techniques to exploit the phone-in format in order to make popular radio.

Another very important example of the phone-in in British radio was the daily morning show on LBC presented by Brian Hayes (1976–1990). Hayes was a controversial and opinionated presenter who brought at least something of the flavour of the US talk radio 'shock jock' to the UK. He was an advocate of the phone-in and argued that it made radio a more democratic medium than any other (Shingler and Wieringa, 1998: 118). There can be no doubt that unlike most news and current affairs, the radio phone-in does allow for the expression of a variety of views and so does contribute to the mediated public sphere. The reality is, however, a good deal more complicated. First of all, although potentially anyone can call, only a very few, unrepresentative listeners, do. There is also a tight vetting of callers to make sure that those chosen are 'appropriate' for the pro-gramme. In addition, the presenters of phone-ins are always in control, 'the centrality of the presenter in the phone-in sequence is not negotiable' (Starkey, 2004: 83). This is particularly well illustrated in a highly influen-tial analysis of the *Tony Blackburn Show* on BBC Radio London. Blackburn's 'discursive kingdom' allowed callers fleeting entry provided they played by the rules. Anyone who strayed from what Blackburn wanted was 'summarily dispatched' (Brand and Scannell, 1991: 213).

Another way of critiquing the belief that the phone-in is in any way empowering is to see the content of much commercial radio as inherently ideological, as a means of promoting consumerism. Australian research found that callers were often conveying the message that 'life was tough' but the message of the station was a brash and positive blend of commercials, music and the optimistic banter of the presenter (Higgins and Moss, 1982). The phone-ins were disempowering, not empowering as they trapped lis-teners and callers in a false consumerist dream.

The connection between the mobile phone and the radio studio is one which is clearly full of potential. Now it is the case that the listener on the street can speak directly to the radio station as a 'citizen journalist'. This is of course particularly valuable for reporting dramatic news events and calls from mobiles played an important part in reporting events like 9/11 and the terrorist attacks in London. Sports fans can also phone up radio stations and report on the match they have just seen, a technique frequently used in the popular BBC Radio Five Live phone-in programme, 606. For the first time in British radio, the voices of listeners have become an essential ingredient in both sports and news coverage on a station such as BBC Radio 5 Live. 'Because phone-in comments from listeners are a staple of the station's diet, they can be used to bolster coverage of breaking news, without seeming incongruous. This extra dimension can add perspectives that enrich the output at little cost to the BBC' (Starkey, 2004b: 35).

The mobile phone offers particularly interesting potential for the future of radio, both as a receiver but also as the source of comment and experiences. In her discussion of the mobile phone, Bassett claims that the mobile fetishises a form of life 'operating at a particular speed and intensity' (2003: 351). The mobile user is not embedded in the locality, in a particular physical space, but connected to people in other locations around the world.

> This change in space means that today I can walk here in the streets and simultaneously connect with other people in far away spaces. I find new perspectives, and not only because I can be reached on my mobile phone but also because I can use it to reach out. (Bassett, 2003: 345, original emphasis)

The enormous connective potential of the mobile phone is reminiscent of the wonder expressed at the possibilities of radio and its ability to allow us to talk to people around the world. Radio and mobile telephony, therefore, share in their use of sound to communicate over distance, but in the latter there is something particularly intense and exciting: 'mobile spaces compel attention because they produce an accelerated, intensified, sense of freedom of movement and of speed-up – a sense that might spill over from the phone space into others spheres of life' (Bassett, 2003: 350). Little surprise then that mobile users might want to speak to a yet wider audience by phoning a radio station and so allow their experiences to spill into a more public sphere.

This entry suggests that the phone-in has made a major difference to the potential and the popularity of radio. Despite the critique of the ideological nature of phone-ins there is plenty of evidence that the opportunity to phone the radio station can be empowering and can also increase the range of voices and opinions expressed. As listeners we are attracted to the opportunity to listen in to what others have to say and this can, especially in the hands of a skilled presenter, be genuinely rewarding and entertaining. As mobiles also become radio receivers the opportunities of extending the communications web and the connectedness of people are greatly increased.

FURTHER READING

Crisell (1994: 189–200) spends some time reflecting on the radio phone-in. For a more recent discussion I would recommend Starkey (2004b). The question of the mobile or cell phone and its relationship to radio is addressed in Bassett (2003).

Podcasting

> **Podcasting refers to producing, and uploading onto the Internet, audio files to be heard using MP3 players.**

The creation of MPEG Audio Layer 3 (MP3) technology at the turn of the century made it possible for people to download and transfer sound files from the Internet, often for no charge. The initial impact of this new technology was in its direct threat to the music industry. The illegal file sharing website Napster encouraged users to download free music, much to the horror of record companies. Eventually Napster was forced out of business, but in 2004 Apple® brought their immensely popular MP3 player, the iPod®, on to the market, which put MP3 technology at the heart of sound media.

The iPod®, and the phenomenon of listening to downloaded sound files, clearly has important implications for radio. First, the iPod® poses a serious threat to music radio because it offers such a flexible and consumer-driven alternative. Why listen to a DJ playing the station's playlist when you can listen to anything at all from your own music collection? Does the iPod® signal the end of music radio, or as Richard Berry puts it, 'will the iPod[®] kill the radio star?' (Berry, 2006). Alternatively does MP3 technology offer the potential for a new form of broadcasting, in other words for 'podcasting', which may help radio to reach new audiences?

As a device for playing music on the move, the iPod® has enabled users to create what Bull calls a 'personalised soundworld' (2005: 343). His research on iPod® use reveals the way people create their own privatised auditory bubble as they listen to the songs they have selected while negotiating the often alienating space of the city. 'Technologies like the Apple[®] iPod[®] produce for their users an intoxicating mix of music, proximity and privacy on the move' (Bull, 2005: 344). The iPod® becomes a tool for carving out a little bit of personal space by allowing the user to listen to the music which they have chosen. There is a striking contrast in Bull's analysis between the uniform and alienating urban backdrop to people's lives and the intensely personal nature of their listening:

> Privatised and mediated sound reproduction enables consumers to create intimate, manageable and aestheticised spaces in which they are increasingly able and desire to live. (2005: 347)

There is something profoundly unradio-like about this description of listening to the iPod®. The orthodoxy of radio studies insists on describing radio listening as a profoundly *social* act. For example, Scannell's references to 'co-presence' and the role of the presenter in achieving this (Brand and Scannell, 1991) or Douglas on the way listening helped fashion generational, gender and national identities during the 20th century (Douglas, 1999). The literature referred to in the book you are reading is full of references to the way that live radio in particular built and positioned its audience and encouraged in them a sense of collectivity. But the iPod® user in Bull's view is almost entirely focused on themselves. They deliberately exploit the potential of the iPod® to turn in on themselves and attend to their own thoughts, moods, reflections and memories – 'being warmly wrapped up in their own personalised space' (Bull, 2005: 349).

The counter argument to this pessimism, at least as far as radio is concerned, is provided by Berry. For him the iPod® is more opportunity than rejection and indeed this has become the mantra of the British radio industry faced by the potential threat that the iPod® offers. Berry's optimism lies in the potential for speech podcasting. For relatively little cost, a listener can become a radio producer and podcast their own audio output. This seems to fulfil Brecht's vision in 1930 of the potential for a truly democratic radio:

The radio would be the finest possible communication apparatus in public life, a vast network of pipes. That is to say, it would be if it knew how to receive as well as to transmit, how to let the listener speak as well as hear, how to bring him into a relationship not isolating him. (Brecht quoted in Berry, 2006: 147)

Building on the success of the web log ('blog') which allowed people to communicate creatively to an Internet audience, podcasting opens up an opportunity to radio amateurs which has been largely denied to them since the birth of broadcasting in the 1920s. There is a danger that all that is produced is the work of the highly esoteric amateur, and Berry acknowledges the amount of podcasting by outspoken evangelists, ego-maniacs, pornographers, audio artists and others. But at least this is radio that has not been censored, it is 'gatekeeper free' technology and all the more stimulating and varied for that. Some of the most successful podcasts are made for niche audiences and provide for a specific need; travel guides for cities and countries, political campaigning speeches and messages and educational podcasts have all been very successful. Comedy is also well suited to podcasting and at the time of writing (2008) the podcasts by the British comic Ricky Gervais have been the most popular podcasts of all.

The mainstream radio industry in the UK has seen the potential of podcasting and used it to 'time shift' programmes and forms of output. The BBC has been at the forefront of this use of podcasting to repackage its output. Speech programmes including *In Our Time, Fighting Talk, The Reith Lectures* and the *Today* programme have all been re-released in MP3 format. The attraction of the podcast to broadcasters is in the potential to give added life to programmes and edited output. The podcast audience becomes an added statistical factor in the measurement of the radio audience, which may help to bolster listening figures.

As a radio optimist, Berry (2006) sees the potential in this new technology to encourage the largely young iPod® users to 'regain the radio habit.' In the particularly telling words of one of Berry's interviewees, the podcast can change 'who's talking and who's listening'. To purists this may not necessarily be radio as we have known it but that seems a slightly sterile debate. The important thing may be that a previously lost generation of listeners to speech output in particular might be attracted either to the brave new world of amateur or esoteric podcasts or to speech radio itself, on their iPods®, on their digital radio or through an integrated mobile phone/MP3 player/radio.

podcasting

43

This is clearly a rapidly developing area but for some early thinking about the podcast there are two very readable and important contributions by Berry (2006) and Bull (2005).

Recording

> *The capture of sounds (including speech), either on location or in the studio, for use in radio programming.*

Radio output can broadly be divided into three categories; pre-recorded, live and 'as live'. The meaning of the first two is fairly obvious but 'as live' refers to radio output that although it sounds as if it is being created at the moment we hear it, was in fact pre-recorded; it has the quality of 'liveness'. It follows that there is rather more recorded output on radio than appears to be the case. An interview in a speech magazine, for example, or even the chatty presentation of a DJ may have been recorded but that fact is hidden. The reason why 'liveness' is valued is discussed in the **liveness** entry and the purpose here is to discuss the development of recording technology and its impact on radio.

In both the USA and Britain, the introduction of recorded programming was partly the result of commercial necessity. In the USA, the formation of the networks in the 1920s encouraged the recording of programmes by affiliate stations for play-back at a different time, important given the different time zones across the continent. The technology for recording was in its early stages and only 15 minutes of sound could be recorded on large aluminium discs. In Britain in the 1930s, commercial stations like Luxembourg and Normandy began to use programming pre-recorded in London and then broadcast from abroad, as Street explains:

> ... up to this time, radio had been principally a 'live' medium, but as the influence of commercial radio grew, and sponsors demanded more famous

personalities to take part in increasingly sophisticated popular broadcasts, recorded programming became the mainstay of output. (Street, 2006a: 115)

Perhaps the most famous of these recorded programmes was *The League of Ovaltineys*, made in London and recorded on the soundtrack of ordinary 35-mm film (as used in the film industry) and then exported for broadcast by Radio Luxembourg on Sunday evenings (Street, 2006a: 112). In the BBC, historically always slower to adopt new technologies, the need to use recording technology grew in the 1930s with the development of the Empire service and so the need to 'bottle' programmes for dispatch abroad (Street, 2006a: 134).

It was not only the need to transport whole programmes from one place or time zone to another that encouraged the use of the new technology. There was also a growing awareness in the 1930s among producers that recording could create new, better and more exciting radio:

> ... within the BBC the pressure grew from journalists, and drama and features producers to develop a technology which could respond creatively to a sense of place, and hold the 'live' moment. The idea of capturing actuality, the eye-witness account, the sense of an event, became increasingly a vital factor in what made radio journalism different to newspapers, and the same idea of getting 'fresh air into the microphone' also influenced writers and producers of drama and features in the latter art of the decade. (Street, 2006a: 134)

This desire for actuality was to be satisfied as a result of the need to report on the Second World War, a powerful catalyst for change in the BBC. There was a growing realisation, reflected in the quote above, that the public needed to hear what was happening on the battlefront and preferably to hear first-hand reports and even the sounds of battle. BBC reporters used mobile recording vans, which at first only allowed three minutes of recording on portable discs. Once recorded the discs were rushed back to a place of safety where the report could be beamed to London for use in the news (Nicholas, 1996: 204). In this way, wartime reporters like Richard Dimbleby managed to convey the sounds and drama of the war. By 1943, portable disc recorders made it possible for a recording to be made inside a bomber over Berlin and then later to record the Normandy landings. Meanwhile, on the other side of the enemy lines German engineers were developing and using magnetic tape recording. When the British army overran the Deutsche Grammophon factory in Hamburg they discovered Hitler's speeches on magnetic tape, 'stored for the posterity of the Third Reich' (Street, 2006a: 133).

After the war, the BBC was comparatively slow to convert from disc to magnetic tape. In 1951, all sound recording was on disc but in 1952 it had six EMI Midget recorders. The impact of tape recording on early current affairs broadcasting, to take just one example, was slow to have effect, but it had the potential to solve many problems, including the need to get enough up-to-date and interesting source material. Recording allowed unscripted discussions to be controlled and used effectively in a magazine format and producers realised that taping discussions allowed them to remove hesitations and repetitions in interviews. Tape recording also greatly increased the quantity of programme material available. Journalists could provide commentary and interviews from around the world and greatly improve the variety and topicality of programme content. Indeed, by facilitating a move to more actuality, recording took production increasingly away from the studio and thereby undermined the increasingly old-fashioned live radio talk.

It is interesting that not everyone in radio embraced the arrival of recording. It may be convenient and the source of huge amounts of new material but for some recorded sound was *inferior* to live radio. Street quotes Briggs on this view, which was common in the post-war BBC:

> 'Live' broadcasting was greatly preferred, almost on moral grounds, to recorded broadcasting: it suggested to the listener, 'this is it'. Suggestions were made also that at the other side of the microphone if artists knew they were being recorded and retakes would be made, they would give mediocre performances. (quoted in Street, 2006a: 118)

Despite this view, recording became increasingly common in radio. Understanding the importance of this development requires thinking about radio's qualities and strengths. One of these is undoubtedly to broadcast the voice of ordinary people, to be a 'democratic' medium that goes beyond the voices and views of the elite. The voice of the people or 'Vox Populi' ('Vox Pop') as it is commonly known was at the heart of the pre-war American programme *Vox Pop*, first broadcast in 1932. Without recording technology this was no mean feat: 'dangling a microphone on a long wire out of the window of radio station KTRH in downtown Houston, the hosts stopped unsuspecting passersby and peppered them with questions – live, uncensored, and on the air' (Loviglio, 2005: 47). The invention of the genuinely portable tape recorder complete with relatively cheap tape made this attempt to record ordinary voices a good deal easier. In Britain the innovative radio producer Charles Parker used recording to capture the unscripted and everyday speech of working class people in particular (what is sometimes referred to as the 'vernacular'). Fifty years later, the use of sound recorders continues to make it possible for the views of people 'on the street' to be used in radio programming and so contribute to radio's democratic potential.

In the last 10 years or so the technology of sound recording has gone through a dramatic period of change. Reel-to-reel tape recorders were initially replaced by digital audio tape (DAT) at the end of the 1980s and then minidisc (MD) recorders replaced DAT. MD recorders were exceptionally light, portable and cheap. At the time of writing, the solid-state recorder has become the industry standard in the UK. This digitisation of recording technology is reflected in the radio studio, where solid-state recording and greatly improved digital playback systems are common. These changes have occurred in tandem with the introduction of digital editing which takes place on the computer screen where a visual representation of the waveform of the audio is used to make editing decisions.

Today, much of the very best output of speech radio is recorded (see the entries on **Documentaries and Features** and **Drama**). Producers are able to select and combine a variety of sounds in a particularly imaginative and creative way, almost to 'compose' radio using modern recording and editing techniques. The pre-recorded programme can be the closest radio comes to being an art but it should not detract from those other essential qualities and strengths of radio; its liveness, intimacy and immediacy – the qualities of unrecorded live radio.

FURTHER READING

For a recent description of sound recorders see Starkey (2004: 1–24). Harman (2004) provides a technologically based history of recording with an emphasis on developments in the studio. The most interesting historical account of recording and its impact on radio is to be found in Street's (2006a) account of British radio between 1922 and 1945.

recording

Serials and Soaps

> *Radio soaps (or serials) are long-running dramas which played a very important part in the early development of American radio.*

The contemporary student of the media is familiar with the importance of the long-running television drama serial or 'soap opera' (usually shortened to 'soap'). Much has been written about the television soap, if only because of its huge importance in the schedule; at the time of writing the top five most popular programmes on British television were all soaps. But the radio equivalent is now seen as a rather archaic phenomenon and examples of it are, though interesting and important in themselves, hard to find. The soap may have largely disappeared from radio but its origins, like its name, are to be found in 1930s American radio (see also the entry on **Drama**).

In their influential, separate accounts of US radio in the 20th century, Hilmes and Douglas both deal, unsurprisingly, with similar themes. It is interesting to note, however, that Hilmes sees the radio soap, its genesis and mode of production, its largely female creators and audience, as worthy of detailed discussion. Douglas, on the other hand, barely mentions the radio soap, choosing instead to focus on comedy, sport and music. This is perhaps symptomatic of the genre; for some the soap is a critical example of what radio does best, the creation of the intimate, often feminised, everyday world of the soap, but for others it is something of an irrelevance.

Soaps first appeared on US radio at a time when a real conflict existed between the populism of advertising-driven radio typified by radio comedies (including *Amos 'n' Andy*) and popular music, and the large radio networks with their 'high culture' pretensions (reminiscent of the BBC at the same time). Advertising agencies began to see the potential of radio to reach mass audiences, and in particular women, providing the content was sufficiently popular. This explains why a type of programming which spoke to women's interests and concerns began to take over day-time radio.

Clara, Lu and Em began in 1930 as an evening comedy sketch show performed by three young women who had recently graduated from

Northwestern University (Hilmes, 1997: 151). There were three characters in the largely improvised show, including a mother of five with an unreliable husband.

In 1931, *Clara, Lu and Em* joined the NBC Blue line-up at 10:30 each weeknight, sponsored by Super Suds detergent – indeed the first soap opera. In 1932 it moved to daytime, sponsored by Colgate, thus representing the first daytime serial drama now understood to be specifically for women audiences (Hilmes, 1997: 109). What followed was the extraordinary takeover of day-time radio by the soap, by 1936 55.3 per cent of the daytime schedule consisted of serial dramas.

The early soaps, and indeed this is arguably a feature of all radio and television serial dramas to some extent, focused on the lives of women and were explicitly targeted at a female audience. As Barnard points out, there was a close link between the early radio soap and women's magazine fiction (2000: 115). Themes of infidelity, life choices (often whether or not to marry), motherhood, unreliable husbands, estrangement and divorce were often featured. Women were frequently represented as strong and dominant and men were marginal characters if they appeared at all. Above all the soaps connected with their huge female audiences by reflecting their concerns.

> Under cover of day-time, women addressed the issues confronting them during the conflicted decades of the 1930s and 1940s, especially the tension between the enforced domesticity of the 1930s and women's increased frustration with this limited role, in forms developed specifically for this purpose and least likely to be penetrated or understood by the executives and critics whose discourse dominated mainstream radio reception (Hilmes, 1997: 154).

There is clearly a tension here (and one which also exists in television studies) between interpretations of soaps that stress their feminist, liberalising qualities and those which see them as reinforcing a woman's domestic role. For advertisers and executives the radio soap produced a captive audience of domestic consumers and preferably one that would not challenge the role of women as the principal consumers of domestic products. Hilmes's emphasis is rather more on the empowering potential of the soap both in terms of the audience but also in the dominant role of women producers. The soap can be seen as a 'subaltern counterpublic' to the essentially masculine public sphere (see the entry on **Gender**). What women producers and writers did was to use the serial drama as a space in which to make 'women's issues' open for public discussion. The production process for these soaps was factory-like in its scope and organisation. Stories were largely scripted by women who worked in teams on very long-running shows like *Road of Life* (1937–1959) and *The Right to Happiness* (1939–1960).

The early soaps were a highly feminised stretch of the schedule and, perhaps unsurprisingly, they were disparaged as melodramatic and frivolous by the male cultural establishment drawn to the higher cultural terrain of night-time radio. If the soaps were seen as women's radio then the more lofty ambitions of, to take the most famous example, Orson Welles' *Mercury Theatre of the Air*, were a more masculine concern. Indeed, Welles was encouraged to work on radio by the CBS network partly to counter the perception of members of the Roosevelt administration that radio was becoming excessively populist and commercial. This view was particularly associated with the day-time soap about which Sidney Strotz, head of NBC's Chicago Bureau, wrote, 'it panders to the crude emotions of the shopgirl type of listener, and it trades upon the maudlin sympathies of the neurotic who sits entranced before the radio, clutching a copy of "True Confessions" and (possibly) guzzling gin and ginger ale' (Hilmes, 1997: 157).

The radio soap did not survive the advent of television, although the television soap maintained the sub-genres, codes, conventions and production routines created for radio. Many of the most popular radio soaps made the transition to television together with their producers (for example, *The Goldbergs* after 20 years on radio was taken by its creator, Gertrude Berg, on to television for a further 10 years).

The British history of serial dramas could hardly be more different from the American one. The high cultural, public service values of pre-war radio, together with notions of 'mixed programming', made a routinised programme like a radio soap an impossibility. The war, however, created much greater flexibility in the BBC and the expansion of the radio networks from one to three created greater space for less highbrow content. It would be hard to overstate the iconic position of the first, and perhaps last, British radio soap, *The Archers*, which began on the Midland Region in 1950 and remains to this day one of the most popular programmes on BBC Radio 4 with six daily episodes of 15 minutes, all repeated daily, and a weekend omnibus (a total of three broadcasts per episode). This 'everyday story of country folk' owes its extraordinary longevity to a strange fact about British society, that although the large majority of the population are urban dwellers and know little about the countryside, British identity is often bound up with the rural way of life.

For them *The Archers* provides an insight into the world of foxhunting, foot and mouth disease and organic food production and of village cricket and a pub full of 'regulars'. The programme has always had an agricultural story advisor, which helps give it a greater authenticity and revolves around the Archers, a family of farmers. An anachronism, but an extraordinarily successful one, on British radio.

Before the arrival of format music radio and the near obliteration of anything else (with some exceptions, including talk radio in the USA and public service radio in Britain) the radio soap was highly successful. That success was partly due to the sheer novelty of a genre that gave women a voice and addressed their concerns. There is also another reason for the temporary popularity of the genre that relates to its *radiogenic* properties (see the entry on **Radiogenic**). As Scannell (1996) has pointed out, radio scheduling, the timing of programmes, reflects the rhythms of the day and also reinforces them. 'Breakfast' shows both fit the mood and activity of the listener having breakfast but also serve to embed 'doing breakfast' as a natural part of everyday life. Breakfast, 'drive time', 'weekend' are in a sense ideological constructs which pattern and restrict everyday life, and radio plays an important part in that construction. A similar point is made by Ellis in his influential discussion of the fragmented 'flow' of television, mirroring the domestic routine (2000). The temporal everydayness of radio is a very important feature and adds to its popularity and relevance for its listeners. This has implications for radio soaps because they have the potential not only in their subject matter to echo the everyday domestic concerns of listeners but also in their reassuringly fixed place in the schedule and in the creation of a fictional world in which time passes in exact parallel with the real world (Hendy, 2000: 184).

This leaves us with an interesting conundrum. The radio soap is, potentially at least, a highly radiogenic genre. Fitting snugly into the schedule it could mark time with the listeners' lives and reflect their intimate concerns. It could, but it does not, because the radio soap has all but disappeared. That it has survived in one or two places, and indeed is very successful where it survives, is testimony to its special radiogenic qualities. The absolute dominance of the visual in dramatic productions, however, whether on film or television, has almost wiped out this form of production – almost but not quite. There are some good examples in African radio (and no doubt elsewhere) of radio soaps being used for development purposes. Messages of AIDS awareness, health, nutrition and agricultural practice can be conveyed using the form of the radio soap.

FURTHER READING

As the radio soap is a largely defunct genre, and even where it does exist it is generally vilified, the literature is unsurprisingly sparse. Fortunately, Hilmes' fascinating and detailed account of the American pre-war radio soap (1997: 150–82) is almost all a student needs.

Sport

Sport radio is a genre and a format based on live coverage of sporting events and follow-up discussion, analysis and phone-ins.

There is a contradiction in the very idea of sport on radio; given the physical nature of sport and its highly visual quality; how can it succeed on this invisible medium? There are no words uttered, or at least few that we can hear, in a sporting contest and the sounds, such as they are, are usually drowned out by the roar of the crowd. And yet the marriage of radio and sport has been so complete that Susan Douglas claims that 'sports on the air may have been the most important agent of nationalism in American culture in the 1920s and 1930s' (1999: 200). Indeed, the history of radio is intertwined with stories of sports coverage, commentators, outside broadcasts and dedicated listeners. How can we explain why these two unlikely partners are so close?

Early experiments with sports coverage on the BBC in the 1920s were severely hampered by the anxieties of the newspaper publishers. There was understandable concern that newspaper sales would be damaged by BBC radio reports of sporting events. As a result, the first experiment in radio sport was a sound-only (commentary-free) report of the Epsom Derby. Unfortunately, it had rained all day, 'and during the race, not only were there no sounds from the hoofs in the soft going, but even the bookies, tipsters and onlookers were more occupied in taking shelter under their umbrellas than in speeding home the winner' (*BBC Yearbook* quoted in Scannell and Cardiff, 1991: 25). The granting of a charter to establish the BBC lifted this censorship and 1927 saw a series of sporting 'firsts' including the first rugby match, the first football (soccer) match, soon followed by regular coverage of other sporting occasions; test match cricket, the annual Oxford and Cambridge Boat Race, Wimbledon and so on.

As Scannell and Cardiff explain, the pre-war BBC was fashioned by Reith and others in the role of guardian and synthesiser of national culture. A sense of national identity was fabricated in the early part of the 20th century by a number of different institutions of which the BBC was pre-eminent. Radio in the 1920s and 1930s, 'made the nation real and tangible through a whole range of images and symbols, events and ceremonies, relayed to audiences direct and live' (Scannell and Cardiff, 1991: 277). Over the years a calendar of events was created which marked out the passing of time with religious festivals (Christmas and Easter), saints' days and other celebrations, and, importantly, events from the sporting calendar.

In the USA, sport started on radio a few years earlier than in the UK. The first baseball game was broadcast in 1921 (Pittsburgh Pirates versus the Philadelphia Phillies) and in the same year the boxing contest between Dempsey and Carpentier began what became a wildly popular form of radio. The popularity of these two sports helped to establish the medium and to create huge audiences, sometimes measuring tens of millions of listeners. By 1942, there were 25 million regular listeners to baseball on radio and it is estimated that two thirds of all radio sets were tuned to hear Joe Louis defeat Max Schmeling in 1938.

The skill of the early radio sports commentators was extraordinary. They fully exploited the medium with their relaxed or excited, colloquial, dramatic and evocative commentaries. These were frequently invented without actually seeing the game. It was much cheaper to pay for a Morse code account of a baseball game (courtesy of Western Union) than actually send a commentator to wherever it was played. The 'announcer' would then use his imagination to fabricate the excitement of the play from a ticker tape with the support of the occasional sound effect (Douglas, 1999: 210).

Sport on radio in the USA, according to Douglas, played an important part in helping to define and reinforce American and male identities. The US population in the 1920s was highly diverse and a significant percentage of the population was born abroad. What it was to be an American and whether there was a need for some form of Americanisation were questions asked at the time. One solution lay in the enthusiastic response to sport on radio. Fans from different backgrounds united in their support for a local or national team and also learned to appreciate the importance of rules and 'fair play'. Sport embodied patriarchal and democratic values and helped to bring them from the public into the domestic sphere. When the great African American boxer Joe Louis knocked out the German Max Schmeling, black and white fans were united by a victory that seemed to symbolise democratic values as well as America's claim to embody toughness and virility. These were attractive and pertinent qualities for American men feeling emasculated by the Depression.

Sport, and especially the types featured on radio, has always been a predominantly male activity. For Douglas, the act of listening to sport on radio did much to articulate American masculinity at a time of great anxiety over what it meant to be a 'real man' (1999: 66). Radio sport did not just represent masculinity in the form of the boxer's brutal strength. Sport gave the listener different models of masculinity. The strength and determination of the boxer (whether he was white or black), the talent, cunning and dexterity of the baseball player and the verbal mastery and wit of the sports announcer. Men also learned the values and mores of rule following, deference to authority, contained aggression, competitiveness and fair play. Fathers and sons bonded together around these values as they listened to the fight or game. Douglas argues that the sports announcer was particularly important in offering a nuanced and diverse representation of masculinity:

> In individual broadcasts, from moment to moment, these men ranged over a broad emotional terrain in a way that simply wasn't permitted in the office or on the shop floor and that offered men a variety of personas to inhabit. Ironically, in listening to something rugged like sports, an act which in itself confirmed one's manhood, one could let loose and verbally and physically express joy, elation, worry, hope, despair, and a deep attachment to others without being feminised. (1999: 217)

It could be argued here that Douglas is overstating the influence of sport radio on masculine identity but it is certainly true that sport does offer men a licence to display a range of emotions which are normally proscribed because they are perceived as feminine.

Much has been written, at times with a distinctly nostalgic enthusiasm, about pre-war radio sport, but the genre and format also remain surprisingly healthy in the television age. Although television is awash with live coverage of golf tournaments, football matches, baseball, tennis and so on, radio has adapted to compete and a lot of its success is due to the skill and techniques of live radio sports commentary. The BBC's *Test Match Special* has provided live coverage of every ball bowled in cricket test matches in England since 1957. The famous cricket commentator and poet John Arlott epitomised the skill of the radio sports commentator in his ability to both describe and 'read' the game; in his case done with a poetic use of language ('you can hear the sighs come out of the spectators like punctured bicycle tyres', 'the trees away in the distance heaving under this strong wind', 'every Englishman in the ground with him. Every West Indian after his blood' (John Arlott in Crisell, 1994: 131). Football coverage on BBC radio is a very different affair. Since 1994, BBC Radio 5 Live has combined news and sport in a highly successful mix. Football is at the heart of the programming and this includes not only live commentary of Premiership games but also a great deal of sports news and discussion, most notably the very popular phone-in, *606*. Because sport is a largely working-class game in the UK and because, unlike most other aspects of British culture, it is particularly strong outside London and the south of England, football coverage often utilises a variety of working-class and regional accents. The experience of listening to sport on 5 Live could hardly be more different than listening to the predominantly middle-class, southern accents of BBC Radio 4. This has given the network a richness, which extends to its **phone-ins**. *606* benefits greatly from the mobile phone used by football fans who, either elated by a win or despondent because their team has lost, phone on their way home from the match. The result is almost a celebration of 'fandom' and of the regional accents of the callers and their unquestionable working-class credentials; a very pleasant contrast to so much of the rest of BBC radio.

In his discussion of live football commentary on BBC radio, Tolson notes, following Crisell on cricket commentary, that the commentator not only describes the game but also provides comments which 'read' the game for the listener (2006: 104). So whether a side is performing well, benefiting from the new manager, lacking the right strategy and so on is all provided in the commentary. In addition, the comments may be related to a 'meta-narrative' of broader themes (for example the decline of skills in English football, the incompetence of referees, the large number of foreign players in the game) which may then feature in the following discussion and phone-in programmes.

Tolson also compares football commentary on radio and television. He suggests that television coverage is more cerebral and analytical whereas sport on radio is an excited, collective experience. The radio listener is positioned as a fan somewhere in the crowd, sharing the experience with the commentator (Tolson, 2006: 112). A defining feature of radio football commentary is the exchange between the commentator and the specialist 'summariser', often a famous former player or manager. This creates a clever conceit that both presenters are in the crowd together with the listener. This is why in radio football commentary direct speech is not used but instead the informal interactive banter of two spectators which the listener overhears.

The success of BBC radio sport and the national commercial station talkSPORT is reflected in the USA where niche sports radio has proved to be not only very popular but also extremely profitable. In New York, WFAN is a specialist sport and sports news station, which also has the talk radio star Don Imus presenting a morning show. The comparatively low cost of sports chat and commentary combined with the affluence of the largely male 25–54-year-old target audience made WFAN the first radio station to earn over US$50 million in commercial revenue. The combination of highly skilled, virtuoso sports announcers and the enthusiasm of sports fans (some listening over the web) means that this radio genre appears to have a healthy future.

FURTHER READING

There can be no question that Douglas on the 'playing fields of the mind' is the single most important contribution to the literature (Douglas, 1999: 199–219). Crisell (1994) is interesting on the coverage of cricket on BBC radio and Tolson (2006) has a fascinating account of sports commentary.

Talk Radio

Talk radio is an American radio format that features a prominent and often highly opinionated presenter (sometimes referred to as a 'shock jock'). Usually combined with phone calls from listeners.

Talk radio is a radio format and an almost exclusively American phenomenon that owes its remarkable success to the specific conditions in the US radio industry. Between 1987 and 2003 the number of talk radio stations in the USA grew from 125 to 1785, often broadcast on AM radio. Talk radio is, as its name implies, speech based and features a prominent or celebrity presenter. Most talk shows include a mix of news, interviews and phone-ins and, that crucial ingredient of the talk format, the strongly held opinions of the presenter.

A forerunner of the talk radio presenter was the infamous Father Charles Coughlin whose diatribes against communism and international banking morphed into attacks on Roosevelt's New Deal in the mid-1930s before their final descent into anti-semitism and apologies for Nazism (see the entry on **Hate Radio**). The modern form of talk radio can probably be traced back to the Jerry Williams-fronted show *What's On Your Mind* on a station in Camden, New Jersey. In the 1960s on KLAC in Los Angeles it was Joe Pyne who added that special ingredient of the format, the outspoken and provocative, 'in-your-face' quality that earned his show the name 'insult radio'.

Rush Limbaugh has probably been the most successful and influential talk radio host. He used his shows to express conservative Republican views and to preach against feminism, environmentalism and liberal causes more generally. Originally he was a fervent supporter of President Reagan and then, with the election of the Democrat Bill Clinton to the White House, he became an outspoken and damaging critic of the Clinton presidency. Limbaugh's success and extraordinary political influence owes a lot to his mastery of the medium of radio. He was a radio DJ at the age of 16 and learned to use talk and sound, satire and sound effects on the radio in a fully developed persona of showman as political guru. He was a demagogue but also a pedagogue in his patient teaching of the audience, 'he brought his listeners into a spectral lecture theatre hall and helped them see themselves as part of a literate community where everyday people, and not just elites, must have knowledge' (Douglas, 1999: 316).

Talk radio has produced some particularly outspoken 'shock jocks' including Howard Stern and Don Imus. Their shows were characterised by obscenity and political reaction, most notably against feminism and liberalism. Stern was opposed to affirmative action policies designed to eradicate discrimination, he decried 'bleeding heart liberals' and 'welfare queens'. Sexist, racist, rude and self-obsessed he displayed the obsessions of the pubescent boy in the locker room. And yet, according to Susan Douglas, Stern was also very funny and in his testosterone-fuelled attacks on feminism he articulated deep male anxieties with his unique, self-deprecating wit. Her account of Stern portrays him as a complex combination of libertarian, liberal and conservative views which were at least refreshingly different from the mainstream media. Stern was a passionate supporter of free speech and believed in talking about sex openly. He also connected with a disenfranchised male audience and the 'sense among many Americans, especially many men, that they were not being addressed or listened to by the mainstream media – that propelled talk radio into a national phenomenon, and a national political force' (Douglas, 1999: 300).

As we see in the statistics above, talk radio really took off in the late 1980s and this extraordinary growth can be explained in three main ways. First, satellite technology introduced in the late 1970s and early 1980s resulted in a modern reinvention of the old radio networks as the syndication of programmes across a range of stations was made possible. These brought the famous celebrity presenters to local stations and also substantially reduced costs. Rush Limbaugh's shows, for example, were aired on 650 stations across the USA in the 1990s. There were also technological developments that made logging calls and communication between presenters and producers easier and quicker. Second, the deregulation of radio in the 1980s, and in particular the Federal Communications Commission's (FCC) abolition of the Fairness Doctrine in 1987, meant that there was no need for political balance in the output of a radio station. One very right-wing presenter could be followed by another one. The expression of largely unrestrained political bigotry became possible, large audiences were listening and so the format spread through the industry.

The third reason for the success of talk radio is to do with its audience and their sense of being politically disenfranchised. The main audience for talk radio has been the white working class. They felt ignored by mainstream liberal media and the comparative anonymity of the radio **phone-in** gave them a place in a populist public sphere (Hendy, 2000: 209). So when Bill Clinton nominated Zoe Baird for the post of Attorney General in 1992 the mainstream media reacted slowly to the revelations concerning her tax avoidance and employment of illegal immigrants for domestic work. Most press and television providers failed to pick up the public mood but talk radio phone-ins were quick to express the outrage felt by 'ordinary Americans' (Hendy, 2000: 208). Mainstream media had become good at expressing the views of the Washington elite but had lost touch with a dissatisfied proletarian audience who saw the world through traditional and conservative American lenses. Talk radio presenters understood that community of listeners and could use great skill and understanding of radio to marshal prejudice and give it a loud and shocking voice.

We are left with other questions about the format which are more difficult to answer. Why is talk radio mainly conservative and anti-liberal? Does the reactionary nature of talk radio matter? A possible answer to the first question is that in the early years of the new format and especially in the 1960s, liberals and progressive deserted radio for the glamour and visual possibilities of television, leaving radio free for the political right to use. Radio is of course not inherently a right-wing medium but the history of radio is full of examples where the voices of the right have found a place which was denied them in other media. As for the overall impact on American democracy there is clearly cause for concern. There has been a debate about the damage that the constant repetition of right-wing prejudices has done to the public sphere. Some people believe that talk radio has fuelled prejudice and, in the words of the *World Press Review*, helped make the US 'a bitter self-doubting nation' (Ellis and Shane, 2004: 1373). The UK has nothing to compare with US talk radio. The regulation of commercial radio and the public service values of the BBC have prevented British listeners from encountering a British Stern or Limbaugh. Whether British audiences are disadvantaged as a result is very much a mater of opinion.

FURTHER READING

For an excellent introductory discussion of issues around talk radio I suggest Hendy (2000: 205–11). Once again, for the definitive account and analysis see Douglas (1999: 284–327), this is a sophisticated and nuanced examination of presenters such as Limbaugh and Stern and highly readable.

talk radio

Part II
Audiences and
Reception

Audience

The term 'audience' is used to discuss both individual listeners and groups of listeners to radio.

All radio is made for an audience, for the mass of listeners who, largely on their own, receive or consume the radio message. Everyone involved today in the business of creating radio has to think about who will listen and this will have a powerful influence on what they make (Hendy, 2000: 115). For historical accuracy it should be said that in the early BBC the wants and desires of the audience were largely ignored in favour of programming that would educate and inform. It was not until 1936 that audience research was established and it was not really till after the Second World War that the BBC began to provide popular entertainment to satisfy audience needs with dance band music and comedy shows on the Light Programme. Commercial radio as been altogether more attentive to its audience and large research organisations (RAJAR in the UK and Arbitron in the US) have provided detailed statistics to satisfy the demand of advertisers for audience statistics.

The physical or spatial dimensions of listening have changed in important ways. The earliest radio listeners used headphones and required a good deal of technical knowledge to operate the equipment. This restricted radio listening to a largely individual and male audience. During the 1920s, valve (or tube) radios were introduced and these bulky items were usually incorporated into a wooden box (see the entry on **Receivers**). It was very much a case of radio moving from the garden shed and into the house. 'To compare receivers from the first and second half of the decade is to see a movement in design away from machines towards furniture. It was an important aspect of the acceptance of radio into the home' (Street, 2002: 29). The domestic and family-based consumption of radio was epitomised by President Franklin D. Roosevelt's *Fireside Chats* of the 1930s and 1940s, which addressed American citizens in their domestic and family unit. From the 1950s radio returned to being a primarily individual medium with the introduction of the transistor and the sale of highly portable and cheap

audience

63

radio sets. Car radios became popular at the same time; adding to radio's reach. The earliest digital radios, often large and heavy but featuring very good sound quality, suggested a return to more traditional static listening but mobile telephony will surely reinforce the listening experience as both individual and portable.

These changes in radio technology have all helped a mass audience for radio to grow and at the same time an audience of potential consumers. Commercial radio stations in effect sell the audience to advertisers and need details such as age, sex and class profile of the audience at any moment in time during the day (see the entries on **Advertising** and **Commercialism**). The larger the audience the greater the income generated for the radio station and as a result commercial radio is unashamedly committed to giving people exactly what they want. Herein lies the rather depressing reason why so much music radio sounds exactly the same; broadcasters have a strong tendency to identify the most lucrative and easy-to-please audience niche (young people who like 'hits') and then use a radio 'format' that targets them. That is why in the USA, contemporary hits radio, classic rock and adult contemporary formats are to be found in every city: UK commercial radio is not that different (Hendy, 2000: 27). This audience-research driven approach to programming also explains why so much effort is put into early morning and late afternoon shows. The peak audiences are to be found as people get up and have breakfast and then later in the day at 'drive time' when they are on their way home. As a result the energy and professionalism of radio at peak time often contrasts disappointingly with what goes on at other times in the day.

So the audience in the commercial radio model is a mass of thousands or even millions of listeners, which is targeted by the radio station with an output designed to please and satisfy. But there is a dilemma here because of the very nature of radio and why people listen to it. As you will read in other entries in this book, radio presenters address the audience as an individual. In British radio this discovery was made by the Head of BBC Talks, Hilda Matheson, in the late 1920s when she realised that someone speaking to a radio audience had to imagine they were talking to an individual, not lecturing to a packed hall. Radio is a domestic medium and so the way they are addressed should 'approximate to the norms not of public forms of talk, but to those of ordinary, informal conversation, for this is overwhelmingly the preferred communicative style of interaction between people in the routine contexts of day-to-day life and especially in the places in which they live' (Scannell, 1991: 4). The dilemma for commercial radio is balancing the model of the audience as a consuming mass while also acknowledging the need to adopt an intimate and personal mode of address.

One of the achievements of radio since the early days has been to establish modes of address that make listeners feel engaged and welcome. The experience of listening to a radio presenter, for example, is not that we are simply the dumb recipients of a one-sided conversation but are somehow interacting with what we hear. The skill, training and use of talk by the presenter all conspire to win over the listener and establish an intimacy in the relationship between the medium and the audience. Douglas adds to this analysis by identifying the socialisation of the listeners into 'modes' or 'repertoires' of listening. If someone grows up listening to radio they can listen to and absorb news and current affairs, or the narrative of a drama, or just take pleasure in the nostalgia of an old hit. They can also take pleasure in the more deviant 'breakout listening', perhaps to a DJ pushing the boundaries or a tirade on talk radio; what Douglas calls a 'transport to a rebellious auditory outpost' (1999: 27).

The radio phone-in adds significantly to the listener's sense of participation, even if they do not phone in themselves. On both speech and music radio stations, the phone-in has become a ubiquitous feature of programming. In recent years this has been enhanced by the use of emails and texts as well as the greater potential of the mobile or cell phone which makes calls from the site of news or sports events possible (see the entry on the **Phone-in**). The phone-in is attractive to the listener perhaps for two main reasons. There is the voyeuristic (or auditory equivalent) pleasure of 'listening in' to a conversation, especially if it is emotionally charged, controversial or funny. In addition we know we have the potential to phone in ourselves:

> Whilst it is true that the phone-in is one of the few radio programme forms which actually allows listeners to interact, the vast majority of the audience of such programmes are content to remain listeners rather than become callers. Therefore, it would be more true to say, that for the majority of the audience listening to phone-ins, such programmes simply represent the possibility or potential of engaging directly in the programme. (Shingler and Wieringa, 1998: 114)

Much has been written at a more theoretical level about how audiences listen to the radio. Douglas provides what is probably the fullest and most useful discussion of the apparently simple act of listening (Douglas, 1999).

She makes an important distinction between hearing and listening: the former is a passive act and the latter an active engagement. We 'hear' all the available sounds around us without necessarily registering them, but when we 'listen' we are consciously engaged in an often pleasurable and imaginative act. She makes a bold claim for the mystical powers of listening, which hark back to a pre-literate, oral culture:

> Because the act of listening simultaneously to spoken words forms hearers into a group (while reading turns people in on themselves), orality fosters a strong collective sensibility. People listening to a common voice, or to the same music, act and react at the same time. They become an aggregate entity – an audience – and whether or not they all agree with or like what they hear, they are unified around that common experience. (Douglas, 1999: 29)

Not everyone will agree with the idea that the unifying power of radio can be traced back to pre-literate society but it is certainly an intriguing claim and one which finds echoes in other writing. The idea that there is something special and unique about listening which is different from the act of seeing is frequently found in writing about radio and the auditory culture. Classen, for example, suggests that in Western culture our senses are culturally constructed so that sight has an objective character often related to science (Tacchi, 2003: 288). In the West sight is equated with scientific understanding and the surface dimension, whereas sound is equated with interior knowledge and a depth of understanding. Using these ideas, Tacchi (2003) suggests that radio has the power to evoke particularly strong feelings of nostalgia, to take one example, in its audience. Nostalgia is an emotional, almost physical, reaction to a stimulus and radio sound can be that trigger.

Many writers on radio point out something paradoxical about listening to radio, and that in this paradox lies the secret of radio's success. For Douglas, radio is both public and intimate. Discussions of the nostalgic quality of some radio, its ability to evoke the past, often relate to this combination of an intensely personal feeling with a healing sense of sharing and collective memory. We are 'taken out of ourselves' but at the same time 'hurled into our innermost thoughts' (Douglas, 1999: 22). Another paradox is the way radio fashions national unity, an imagined community, while at the same time having the potential to celebrate 'a conspiratorial sense of subcultural difference'. Reith would have agreed that radio contributes to national unity; commenting on King George V's speech opening the British Empire Exhibition, the first time the king had been heard on radio, he said that this had the effect of 'making the nation as one man' (Scannell and Cardiff, 1991: 7). But radio has also contributed strongly to the formation of **subcultures**; the creation of youth culture in the 1950s and 1960s owed a lot to DJ-led pop radio.

Any general account of the development of the radio audience is inevitably a history of radio's survival. It will chart adaptations in listening technology, the techniques of the presenter and the modes of listening as culture and the media change over time. From 1927, the year of the Radio Act in the USA and the establishment of the BBC as a public corporation in the UK, the radio audience has continued to listen in large numbers to a medium which has today many of the features established then. But if it really is the case that we are gradually socialised into the full repertoire of listening styles during a lifetime (as so graphically described by Douglas in her account of being a teenager in the 1950s and 1960s) then is this a reason to fear for the future of the radio listener?

FURTHER READING

A good starting point for further reading, if rather UK oriented, is Shingler and Wieringa (1998: 110–17). Loviglio (2005) provides a cultural history of the American audience which includes a detailed look at the *Fireside Chats*. Tacchi's (2003) observations on radio and nostalgia are interesting and contemporary.

Blindness

> *A controversial term used to describe the lack of visual images on radio.*

What strikes everyone, broadcasters and listeners alike, as significant about radio is that it is a *blind* medium. (Crisell, 1994: 3, original emphasis)

With these words, Crisell started the first chapter of his ground-breaking text, *Understanding Radio* first published in 1986. He proceeds to discuss the characteristics of radio as responses to its blindness, as compensatory devices aimed at making good this one fundamental lack. It is worth spending a little time looking at the detail of Crisell's argument, a position that has attracted a considerable amount of criticism.

We can think of radio, he argues, as one example of different modes of communication. Interpersonal communication, for example two people chatting on a street, is both oral and visual. It includes not only speech but also facial expressions, body language and other clues, and takes place in a shared location or context. Furthermore, those participating in the conversation can provide feedback and ask questions which add to the effectiveness of the communication. This can be contrasted with mass communication, which is far more impersonal, there is no feedback possible (or very little) and the message has to contain its own context, to confirm what it is about. Television can solve some of these problems by the use of visual images, which can explain the context without the use of words and convey meaning in their own right. Radio, however, has to rely on auditory 'codes' alone; speech, music, sounds and silence (see the entry on **Codes**):

> The risks of ambiguity or complete communication failure are high, and so in all kinds of radio much effort is expended on overcoming the limitations of the medium, on establishing the different kinds of context which we would generally be able to see for ourselves. (Crisell, 1994: 5)

One of the reasons why radio is defined by the need to compensate for its visual handicap, he argues, is because of a 'hierarchy of the senses' in which sight is top and hearing comes second. Furthermore, hearing often leads to confusion, 'the ear is not the most 'intelligent' of our sense organs' (Crisell, 1994: 15).

According to Crisell, radio compensates for its blindness by the use of 'signposts' and 'framing'; constant statements about what is happening and where and what will happen next, as well as music and other sounds to identify the radio station or the start or end of the programme or the format or genre. But for Crisell, blindness also gives radio some of its strengths. The need to use the listener's imagination creates an engagement that can itself foster a companionship (or intimacy) between presenter and listener. Another by-product of radio's visual disability is its cheapness to produce, which can facilitate a greater variety of programming. Radio is also highly portable and does not require the level of attention demanded by the visual media: it is a 'secondary' medium that can be received while the listener is doing something else.

It is perhaps not surprising that such a strident statement about radio's deficiency, combined with the assertion that all other characteristics flow from it, has been vociferously rejected, in particular by other British radio academics and producers. Most notable is Crook's 'defence' of radio, as he would see it, in a chapter in his book on radio drama entitled 'Radio drama is *not* a blind medium' (1999: 53–70, original emphasis). Crook begins his attack on the blindness metaphor by criticising the very notion of a hierarchy of the senses. The desire to establish such a hierarchy is 'inherently depressing'. He adds that the difference between sight and imagination has not been proved: 'What is the philosophical difference between seeing physically with the eye and seeing with the mind?' (1999: 54). Arguably the most persuasive part of Crook's thesis is his idea that radio stimulates in the imagination not just crude visual representations but the full range of emotions and feelings. These are often augmented by our visual and experiential memories and he quotes a report of the UK Radio Advertising Bureau to support his case, 'the theatre of the mind is an emotional theatre, where feelings are the primary currency, mixed with mood, memories and imagination' (1999: 61). A similar point is made by the British radio producer and director Donald McWhinnie:

> Radio drama does not act as a stimulus to direct scenic representation; that would be narrow and fruitless. It makes possible a universe of shape, detail, emotion and idea, which is bound by no inhibiting limitations of space and capacity. (Cited in Crook, 1999: 66)

Referring to radio drama, Crook argues that the imagination can indeed create the sort of spectacle we normally associate with television or film and that the very idea of blindness is a 'gesture of intellectual and philosophical insecurity'.

Taking a slightly different approach, but no less emphatic and critical of the idea of radio blindness, Shingler and Wieringa take particular exception to the connotations of impairment or disability contained in the word 'blind' (1998: 74). They ask why radio is described by Crisell and others as 'blind' and not 'invisible'. The word invisible could suggest radio's secret power and magic whereas the word blind is bluntly negative. This obsession with deficiency is not shared by the visual arts or by novelists and literary critics. We do not criticise the novel for its lack of pictures or paintings for their 'silence'. Going a step further than other commentators, Shingler and Wieringa claim that radio is a 'visual medium'. Visual because it stimulates the imagination and because the listener has, especially in the case of radio drama, to play an active part in the creation of the programme. At the same time they also accept Crisell's point that the lack of pictures on radio forces the drama producer to limit the complexity of narratives and range of characters in order to avoid confusion.

Crisell's 'blindness thesis' *can* be seen as a rather pointless philosophical exercise, removed from the realities of everyday radio production and consumption. But the debate has a strong subtext in its attempt to identify the unique properties of radio, of radio's defining characteristics and strengths, and Crisell spends more time discussing these than in criticising the medium. There is agreement between him and Shingler and Wieringa that the absence of visual images (no matter how we want to describe this) produces certain special advantages, which go some way to explain why radio survived the advent of television. The **secondariness** of radio means that the listener can easily perform some other activity (work, drive and so on) while listening and paying attention to the radio. More importantly, the radio DJ or other presenter, speaking directly to the listener, can sound more authentic than the television presenter because they are 'undisturbed by the constructedness and artificiality of their production values' (Shingler and Wieringa, 1998: 80). This is an insight that most contributors to this debate would accept, that our inability to see radio presenters (complete with white teeth and carefully groomed hair) is central to the intimacy possible between audience and presenter. As they put it, the unconstructedness of radio personalities makes them seem 'ordinary, everyday, familiar and natural: more like us in fact'.

We may want to differ with Crisell in an argument which at times looks reductionist (reducing all of radio to one key deficiency) and essentialist (seeing radio as having an essence which both defines and undermines it). In the past, sociologists have warned of a tendency to define people with one notable characteristic, 'black', 'Christian', 'female', 'young' and so on, as completely dominated and defined by it. Radio may be 'invisible' but that is only one of *many* characteristics and the use of the word 'blind' is a deliberate sleight of hand to insinuate that this is a disability. In some circumstances it clearly is a disadvantage but to see all radio as limited is to accept the dominance of visual culture without a challenge.

To conclude what might appear to be a rather dry and academic discussion let us turn to the great poet of radio theory and history, Douglas.

She suggests that there is something 'magical' (to use a word also used by Crook) about hearing without seeing. Aurality, listening to speech and music, is a driving force in cultures around the world:

> I don't mean to suggest that listening to Rudy Vallee or Casey Kasem was like a religious experience (although perhaps, for some, it was). I am talking about the medium itself and the way that receivers reel in distant voices out of that incomprehensible dimension called the spectrum and effortlessly bring them straight to us, linking us, through the air, to unseen others. The fact that radio waves are invisible, emanate from 'the sky,' carry disembodied voices, and can send signals deep into the cosmos links us to a much larger, more mysterious order. (Douglas, 1999: 41)

This celebration of the wonder and magic of radio could hardly be further from Crisell's gloomy dissection. This is an important debate, which contrasts a British pragmatism and realism with American nostalgia and romanticism.

FURTHER READING

The necessary starting point for further reading is Crisell's (1994) famous statement about radio's blindness at the beginning of his early text. For a thorough reply I suggest Shingler and Wieringa (1998: 73–93). Another rebuttal of the blindness thesis is provided by Crook (1999: 53–70).

Codes

> *Codes are the categories of sound identifiable in radio output and these are speech, music, noise and silence.*

In his introduction to *Understanding Radio*, Crisell uses the ideas and concepts of semiology, the study of signs, to explain how radio creates meaning. In fact, the semiological approach to radio has not proved popular and there is little, if any, radio semiology. There is, however, an ongoing debate about the related concept of the radio code.

The sounds heard on radio can be categorised as individual elements; a spoken word, a musical note, a cough, the wind blowing and so on. These 'sound signs' can then be grouped into what are generally called radio's 'codes'; speech, music, noise and silence. The different codes are what we might call modes of communication, which carry meaning in different ways. It might be useful to consider a non-radio example of a code: before the invention of radio, the Morse code was used to communicate using a combination of long and short sounds to represent the letters of the alphabet. Famously, the radio pioneer, Guglielmo Marconi, sent the letter 'S' in Morse code across the Atlantic in 1901 (Street, 2002: 14). The letter S is indicated by 'dot dot dot' (…), this is the individual sign for S. For all codes there are individual signs, the meaning of which we as receivers can interpret according to generally agreed rules. Clearly the precision of meaning varies between different codes. Speech is relatively transparent. When the weather forecaster says 'it's raining' listeners know what that means. Other radio codes, however, are less precise and more ambiguous. The sound on radio of a hooting owl can convey a variety of different meanings; the night, the natural world, a sense of foreboding and so on. In addition, the meaning of coded sound partly depends on the identity of the listener. This is particularly true in the case of music. An early Bob Dylan song from the 1960s will mean something quite different to someone who remembered it the first time round (for example signifying the 'peace and love' culture of the time) and something else to a teenager.

Although the different radio codes vary in their degree of transparency, they all make an essential contribution to the exclusively sound medium:

> Without words, radio would be seriously disadvantaged, rendered obscure, ambiguous and virtually meaningless. Nevertheless, without noises and music, radio would lack depth and detail, making it seem sterile, flat and unrealistic. (Shingler and Wieringa, 1998: 51)

We can see in this quote the suggestion that radio's codes are not of equal importance. Indeed, in all of the major introductions to radio studies published in the UK, speech (or language) is referred to as radio's *primary* code. This assertion was first made by Crisell, 'it seems reasonable to suggest ... that the primary code of radio is linguistic, since words are required to contextualize all the other codes' (1994: 54). Shingler and Wieringa are slightly more cautious, 'speech may be the primary code of radio' (1998: 51) and Hendy states that 'talk ... is almost always described as the "primary code" of radio, which contextualizes all other sounds' (2000: 155). Crisell is the most adamant in his argument, stating that speech is essential to provide meaning in radio and that music, in comparison, is almost without meaning, referring to 'the virtual absence of meaning in music' (1994: 49).

There is clearly a risk in proclaiming that speech is the primary code of radio: that somehow speech-based radio is itself more important than music radio. Or that even in music radio the important part is the speech or performance of the DJ and not the music (although this view is reinforced by the availability of podcasts consisting of DJ talk without the music!) It is certainly the case that much of the writing about radio, which constitutes radio studies, has been about speech radio (for example, drama, documentaries and features, news, comedy, phone-ins). As Paul Long points out, even writing about music radio has tended to ignore the music (2006: 28). Not only has radio been devalued as a 'secondary medium'; music has been relegated below speech. He cites the example of Brand and Scannell's (1991) influential analysis of the performance of the Radio London DJ Tony Blackburn. The focus is very much on how Blackburn creates a unique 'discursive world' through the use of speech, there is little on the music played or its contribution to the meaning of the show. Long argues that in the case of the music programmes presented by the iconic and idiosyncratic British DJ John Peel, the music was made the priority:

> The defining characteristic of John Peel's identity and value lay in the obvious yet radical act of prioritising music as the primary code of his form of music radio, built upon an affirmation of its centrality to his very existence and indeed to his audience. (2006: 35)

It could be argued that Crisell and others are not claiming that music on radio is unimportant but rather that music requires speech to contextualise it. To put it differently, that music on radio without any speech would scarcely count as radio at all, an argument which is important for understanding the difference between portable 'music on demand' players like the iPod® and conventional DJ-led music radio.

FURTHER READING

The use of semiology to understand radio is well discussed in Crisell (1994: 42–64). This approach has not been popular in recent years although it is referred to in Long's (2006) important discussion of the work of the British DJ John Peel.

Co-presence

> **Co-presence refers to the idea that radio listening is a sociable activity and that listening simulates being with presenters and other listeners.**

One of the purposes of this book is to take radio, that humble and everyday accompaniment to our lives, and attempt to dismantle and dissect the fundamentals of what it is and what listening means. The simple act of listening to radio carries with it certain connotations actively fostered by the broadcaster but not immediately obvious, in fact not obvious at all. One of the basic facts of radio, that when we listen others are listening too, is worthy of further scrutiny and is related to other concepts in this book including **liveness** and **intimacy**.

The idea of 'co-presence', of the shared experience of radio listening, is one of the most influential and significant concepts in radio studies. It helps us to understand the particular nature of the experience and perhaps the particular strength of the medium and its enduring appeal. To understand the idea it is helpful to look at its origins in British radio studies and in particular the work of Scannell, one of the founders of, and most important contributors to, the subject in Britain. In *Radio, Television and Modern Life* (1996) he was influenced by the work of the German philosopher and phenomenologist Martin Heidegger. Phenomenology is a philosophical perspective that addresses the nature of being: not only what it is to be a person but also the experience of living in the world. Scannell attempted to use Heidegger's insights in an analysis of contemporary broadcast media and its interaction with our daily lives. One of the main ideas emerging from this work is the idea of the shared experience of listening or viewing at the same moment in time and the sense of others being present (or 'co-present') with us in that activity.

In his discussion of the experience of radio listening, Hendy (a former colleague of Scannell's at the University of Westminster) brings together ideas of time, intimacy and 'sociability' (or co-presence). All forms of radio acknowledge the time of day and in the case of music radio the labelling of shows as 'breakfast' or 'drive time' illustrates this well. Drawing on a well established tradition of writing about broadcasting and time (Williams, 1974; Ellis, 1982) Hendy examines the shared experience of listeners moving through the day together, 'our lives stand in the same temporal relation to other listeners as much as they stand in the same temporal relationship to the programme we hear' (2000: 184). This time-based, sociable experience is also characterised by intimacy, that uniquely close relationship between some, if not all, radio and its listeners: 'Time ... and the familiarity engendered over time, is one of the foundations upon which radio's intimacy is built. And not just its intimacy, but its sociability too' (2000: 184). So when we turn on the radio in the morning and gradually wake up to the voice of a favourite DJ or presenter, we share an intimacy at a very precise moment in time with thousands or millions of others and so experience the sociable 'co-presence' of 'being-in-world' (to borrow Heidegger's own expression) along with other listeners.

This attention to the sociability of radio has not only been a British concern. It is significant that in her discussion of 'listening in' the American writer Douglas also discusses co-presence. She does so, however, not with reference to German philosophy but, in a chapter with the exotic title 'The Zen of Listening', she introduces the idea of the 'imagined community' and the work of Benedict Anderson (see the entry on the **Imagined Community**). Anderson was interested in the rise of nationalism at the end of the 19th century and the paradox that there are great passions engendered by nationalism, including the willingness to die for a country, despite the fact that the nation is simply an idea, an 'imagined' entity. In addition, nations are often divided by class and economic inequality so that nationalistic feelings have to overcome not only geographical space but also social divisions. This is all done in the imagination of the citizen. In the historical examples described by Anderson that imagination was partly inspired by the act of reading the newspaper:

> We know that particular morning and evening editions will overwhelmingly be consumed between this hour and that, only on this day, not that. The

significance of this mass ceremony – Hegel observed that newspapers serve modern man as a substitute for morning prayers – is paradoxical. It is performed in silent privacy, in the lair of the skull. Yet each communicant is well aware that the ceremony he performs is being replicated simultaneously by thousands (or millions) of others of whose existence he is confident, yet of whose identity he has not the slightest notion. (Anderson, 1993: 35)

It is hardly surprising that radio scholars like Douglas have seen in this account echoes of the radio listening experience. Anderson describes the newspaper equivalent of the 'liveness' of radio and the co-presence of radio listening. The 'silent privacy' of newspaper reading is reminiscent of radio's intimacy. Much of what follows in her account of American radio in the 20th century builds on the collective experience of different radio audiences at different historical times; the mass audiences listening to baseball in the 1930s and the youth audiences for radio playing Rock 'n' Roll in the 1950s – both forged into imagined communities by their shared experience, by their co-presence, not only as listeners but also with announcers and DJs.

Co-presence is not an accidental by-product of radio, it is a defining characteristic and vital ingredient in the success of the medium and therefore one which is often actively fostered. This is particularly true of music radio. Traditionally, DJs have built not only 'intimacy at a distance' but also a sense of shared identity and experience in their audience. It is obviously very much in the interests of the DJ to bind the audience together and to him/her to keep them listening on a regular basis. Here again we see the interrelationship between intimacy, liveness and co-presence. DJs use direct speech ('I', 'you', 'we', 'our') to encourage a sense of friendship or intimacy and words like 'now', 'here' and 'next' to stress liveness. The overall effect is a sense of community, of belonging to the private/public world of the DJ. In their discussion of the British DJ Tony Blackburn, Brand and Scannell (1991) describe that sense of belonging to a special group of radio fans led by one DJ who shares his own history, thoughts and emotions with his listeners.

One of the most interesting developments in the presentation style of DJs has been 'zoo radio'. In Britain, zoo radio was first introduced in the early 1990s and is often linked to the BBC Radio 1 DJ Chris Evans. Rather than just one presenter, zoo radio includes a DJ together with one or more other participants in a style reminiscent of both the 'shock jocks' of American talk radio and the anarchic experimentation of British 'youth television' (Tolson, 2006: 114). But zoo radio did not supersede more conventional styles, they both work to unite listeners and presenters in one 'discursive kingdom' ruled over by the DJ (see the entry on **DJs and Presenters**). Tolson shows how Chris Evans builds his listening community by analysing a transcript from one of his programmes:

> 'It's five minutes past eight that's the time eight oh five on Friday morning April 26th 1996 the last day that we're here for four weeks (studio cheers) we're out for four weeks (studio: bye) okay there's just one day to go until we see Oasis at Maine Road tomorrow joining us will be you the listeners if you're not going to be at Maine Road you ain't going nowhere you're losing out on a weekend of your life you should have bought tickets you should go to the gig of the century Oasis on Sunday and Saturday. Coming with us Bud, Neil Hawes, Adam Whitely and Lindsay Brown from Chandler's Sixth form College in Ipswich, Jim and Nick in Buckinghamshire …'. (2006: 117)

Several features of this talk are worthy of comment. The sociability and co-presence of the audience is constantly reinforced. Listeners are addressed directly in the plural but also as named individuals, serving to increase the sense of belonging to a club or group of friends. An '**imagined community**' is described but one which is geographically dispersed and has a distinct national (British) identity united behind the phenomenon of the leading 'Britpop' band, Oasis. We should also note Evans' emphasis on the time enhancing the **liveness** of the show and the temporal co-presence of presenter and listeners.

It is possible to place radio's emphasis on community and co-presence in an historical context; from the origins of broadcast radio to the recent direct challenge to live radio from digital forms of audio. The 1930s in both the UK and the USA witnessed the extraordinary rise of radio as a domestic necessity. Then, it was still unchallenged by television that would only start to usurp radio's dominance in both countries after the Second World War. In Britain, in particular, radio's popularity grew at the same time as old working-class communities were broken up and the population started to move into the suburbs. Geographical and social mobility were linked to an increase in the privatised family, finding recreation less in urban pubs and clubs and more often in the privacy and comfort of the suburban house. The claims radio makes, and others make for it, to be able to create imagined communities cannot be divorced from the historical fact that radio rose to prominence at exactly the same time that 'real' physical communities were being destroyed.

Whether or not radio listeners are co-present one with another and with the presenter may appear a rather academic issue. But if co-presence, and the related characteristics, intimacy and liveness, are indeed distinctive qualities of radio and ones which make it successful, then this has serious implications for radio's future. The invention of the portable MP3 player and its ability to play music from a huge cache of songs has been widely described as potentially fatal for commercial music radio and other formats as well. What pre-recorded music lacks, no matter how wide the choice and how convenient and stylish the technology, are the qualities of co-presence, liveness and intimacy described here. But digital media may so undermine collective forms of consumption that the pleasures of imagined communities and the experience of listening live may themselves become an irrelevance.

FURTHER READING

A useful introduction to further reading is Hendy (2000: 149–55, 184–5). Scannell himself has a chapter that examines historical examples of radio sociability (1996: 22–58). The relevance of Anderson's idea of imagined community is to be found in the section with that title in Hilmes (1997: 11–23). A more contemporary account of co-presence is Tolson's (2006: 113–29) analysis of the British DJ Chris Evans.

Hot and Cool Media

> The terms 'hot' and 'cool' media are closely identified with Marshall McLuhan and refer to differing amounts of information available in different media.

The Canadian theorist Marshall McLuhan (1911–1980) was one of the most controversial and iconoclastic thinkers of the 20th century. His writing on the media is rich with often quoted maxims; 'the medium is the message' and 'the global village' being just two of them. Despite writing extensively about the mass media, McLuhan is probably not as widely read today as, for example, the great French media philosophers such as Barthes, Baudrillard and Bourdieu. This comparative neglect may be due to the obscurity and extraordinary range of his writing, which includes a bewildering variety of historical, literary and scientific material. One American academic, George P. Elliott, expresses the frustration that many readers have when they try to make sense of McLuhan:

> It is not possible to gave a rational summary of McLuhan's ideas for two reasons: the attitude and tone of his writing are at least as important as the ideas themselves, and to sytematize these ideas, even in outline, would be to falsify their nature and impact. His writing is deliberately anti-logical: circular, repetitious, unqualified, gnomic, outrageous. (Quoted in Stearn, 1968: 89)

However, McLuhan's writing contains some extremely important and thought-provoking insights into the media and its relationship with society and specifically into the nature of radio. In addition, McLuhan helped make media studies, of which he was an early and founding contributor, a serious academic subject.

McLuhan's early writing addresses different stages of the development of communication media. He describes the pre-literate world as 'the age of acoustic space' where speech was the primary medium. In the 'tribal' world, relationships were more personal and intimate, a quality that was lost by the coming of print and the increasing importance of visual imagery. Print, alongside the development of literacy, is associated with linear, logical thought and its emergence had a profound cultural influence. What is important about this argument is the emphasis McLuhan places on the impact that changes in the communication media have on individuals and their awareness of the world around them. For McLuhan the media (print, speech, radio and so on) are extensions of the central nervous system. As they evolve they fundamentally alter our perception of the world and how we interact. This makes McLuhan a technological determinist, he thought that the technical characteristics of the media fundamentally determined their impact. This helps to explain his somewhat mysterious claim that 'the media is the message'; what he seems to mean here is that what is communicated has less influence than the means by which it is communicated. An idea that is explored in more detail towards the end of this entry.

If we examine McLuhan's ideas for some insight into radio the most obvious area of interest is his theory of 'hot and cool' media. A hot medium is 'high definition', in other words it contains so much information that the receiver has no scope for interpretation. Hot media, therefore, require low participation by the receiver and exclude the audience. In contrast, cool media provide us with meagre amounts of information and so we have to work a bit harder to interpret them. This means that they are more inclusive as we engage more actively with them. For students of the media this is not an unfamiliar argument and the themes of audience activity and passivity have been widely discussed. However, in the case of McLuhan his labelling of different media is perplexing:

Hot media	Cool media
Radio	Telephone
Print	Speech
Photograph	Cartoons
Films	Television
Lecture	Seminar. (Terrence Gordon, 1997: 201)

If we ignore radio for a moment there is clearly a good case for defining lectures as hot and seminars, with their greater engagement but less information, as cool. Similarly, photographs are packed with detail and so are hot, while cartoons often require much more active interpretation and so are cool. The case of both radio and television, however, is rather mystifying. As Hendy puts it, 'his classification now seems rather topsy-turvy' (2000: 1). Today it is television that is perceived as high definition (a term now used to describe its visual density), encouraging passive response from the viewer whereas radio is surrounded by the rhetoric of coolness. The radio studies orthodoxy is that radio is a quintessentially cool medium, spare with its information but inclusive of the listener who actively interprets and engages with radio sound (Crisell, 1994; Shingler and Wieringa, 1998).

Despite the confusions and mystery surrounding McLuhan's work, there is a quality of insight which can help us make sense of contemporary radio, even if not quite in the way that he envisaged. There is no doubt that he is right that different media demand different types of response and that the labels hot and cool are attractive and relevant even if we might want to relabel radio as cool. The idea that the media is the message is also important and contains some insight for students of radio. McLuhan is certainly underestimating the importance of programme content in this claim but the idea that radio's non-visual and auditory nature is important is a useful one. This approach prioritises the act and experience of listening and being a listener above the content of radio broadcasts. Although this is a radical view it reminds us of the importance of the listener and the act of listening in our approach to studying radio.

Similarly, McLuhan's technological determinism is thought provoking. For him, the rise of the electronic media did not just change what people did in their spare time, it fundamentally changed the nature of people's perception and interaction. Radio here is seen not simply in terms of content but as an extension of the individual and radio listening (or watching television, using the computer or the mobile phone) is significant as an act more than for the content of the communication. As Bassett argues about the mobile phone, it changes our experience of the present, our connection to other people in other worlds and our 'always on' accountability (Bassett, 2003: 345). The mobile phone is the message (in a McLuhanite account) not the words spoken. There are interesting connections here between the mobile phone, a relatively new invention, and the early years of radio. The fact of being connected, live, to the community, the nation and even the world was perhaps as important as the content of programmes.

FURTHER READING

There is of course a substantial literature on McLuhan and some of it available online. However, there is probably no harm in trying the original (McLuhan, 1994). Hendy (2001: 1) points out the 'topsy-turvy' nature of McLuhan's theory. Bassett (2003) provides a very interesting McLuhanite account of the mobile or cell phone.

Imagined Community

This refers to the sense of belonging to a defined community (including the nation), which radio and other media are able to foster among listeners.

Both of the most important radio-centric cultural histories of America draw heavily on the concept of the imagined community (Douglas, 1999;

Hilmes, 1997). Similarly, British histories of radio have also referred frequently to the relationship between radio and the experience of feeling a part of a wider group (Hendy, 2007; Scannell and Cardiff, 1991). Despite the influence of the concept on radio studies in its original formulation by Benedict Anderson there is no mention of radio at all. In his attempt to understand the emergence of nationhood in the late 19th century and the subjective experience of belonging to a nation, Anderson examined the role of the press. He suggested that despite the often huge social, ethnic, linguistic and geographical divisions within a nation, the experience of reading the same newspaper every day was profoundly unifying (1983: 35). In effect, the act of reading the national newspaper was a mass ceremony in which everyone who took part knew that there were thousands or millions of others doing the same thing. Even though reading the paper was often a silent and private act it had the effect of building an imagined national community.

As I have mentioned in the entry on **co-presence** it is hardly surprising that radio scholars have seen in Anderson's work on the press echoes of the radio listening experience:

> ... listeners tuning in by the tens of thousands to one specific program airing at a specific time created that shared simultaneity of experience crucial to Benedict Anderson's concept of the modern 'imagined community' of nationhood. (Hilmes, 1997: 11)

Quoting a commentator writing in the early 1920s, Hilmes describes the ambitions early pioneers had that 'radio would unite a far-flung and disparate nation, doing "more than any other agency in spreading mutual understanding to all sections of the country, to unifying our thoughts, ideals and purposes, to making us a strong and well-knit people"' (Hilmes, 1997: 13). It was not simply the act of shared listening that created national and other identities, the content of broadcasts would act to unite listeners in the shared appreciation of culture. In the UK, the BBC defined what counted as culture in decidedly hierarchical terms, with prominence given to classical music, improving talks by experts and large doses of religion. In America, although the 'national culture' was initially defined in terms of the same 'high culture', there were much stronger pressures to reflect popular tastes.

One of the main reasons why the idea of the nation, and radio's contribution to it, was different in the two societies was because of fundamental differences in their social composition. Pre-war Britain was a highly traditional and hierarchical society, complete with a state religion (the Church of England) and a widely respected monarchy (Brendon, 2000: 356). The BBC was led by the arch monarchist and enthusiastically evangelical John Reith. An interesting feature of the symbolic creation and reinforcement of national identity in the early BBC was the use of outside broadcasts. These included religious services, opera, plays, variety performances, dance music, speeches by public figures, ceremonies, events and sport, including football, cricket, racing, tennis and boxing (Scannell and Cardiff, 1991: 278). The imagined community of Britain was fostered by the huge radio audiences sharing this rather rich diet of high cultural content combined with some lighter entertainment, sport and a great deal of solemn religious programming.

America was, of course, a very different society and so was the sense of imagined national identity. The early 20th century saw a great wave of 'otherness' sweep on to American shores (Hilmes, 1997: 25). Thirty million immigrants arrived between 1890 and 1920. America was already a nation with profound racial divisions and the addition of the new, mainly European, immigrants added to the ethnic diversity. As a result, American radio's formulation of national identity both acknowledged, for example, African Americans while at the same time maintaining racial boundaries. In the pre-war comedy show, *Amos 'n' Andy* two white men 'blacked up' in the tradition of vaudeville and the minstrel show (see the entry on **Comedy**). The characters spoke in exaggerated accents and mangled the English language. Their ignorance of the modern, urban world is an important part of the long-running joke. Early American radio, therefore, acknowledged racial differences but did so using the demeaning stereotypes of the minstrel tradition. Even the jazz superstar Louis Armstrong was expected to act in a short comic sketch as well as play music in the 1937 *All Colored Program*. When he refused to speak the minstrel dialogue and changed it to standard English he was labelled 'difficult' and the show was cancelled (Hilmes, 1997: 79). So the imagined community of America in the pre-war period reflected social differences, and far more than on the BBC, but did so in a way that caricatured and demeaned minorities.

A central theme in Douglas's (1999) *Listening In: Radio and the American Imagination* is the way radio played on the imaginations of those who grew up in America at the time when radio was more important than television. Like Hilmes, she acknowledges the two sides of this imagining, 'while radio brought America together as a nation in the

1930s and '40s, it also highlighted the country's ethnic, racial, geographic, and gendered divisions' (1999: 5). She also describes the plethora of imagined communities; sports fans, rock 'n' rollers, jazz fans. The power of sport to create both national but also ethnic solidarity was remarkable. The broadcasting of boxing tournaments in the 1930s was made possible by literally wiring the nation up in a complex system of radio networks and so creating a kind of physical tying together of the listeners. For Douglas, radio's power over the American audience, which made these psychically based communities possible, lay in its non-visual quality, in its 'blindness'. By letting the listener fill in the gaps left by the absence of pictures, radio cast a much greater spell over its audience, who then learned what it meant to be an American, a teenager or a man.

Perhaps the best example of radio in Britain creating the nation in the minds of its listeners is to be found on BBC Radio 4. Appealing to a largely middle-class and middle-aged audience, BBC Radio 4's speech-based programming has come to speak for England on behalf of its fiercely loyal listeners. Hendy describes how even the *Shipping Forecast*, designed for those at sea around Britain's coasts, has come to have a powerful effect on the imagination of listeners, unifying and reinforcing ideas of the nation:

> Here, a sense of nationhood, of belonging to an island community, is contained within. David Chandler, for example, sees in the forecast a 'landscape of the imagination' with a romantic version of the British Isles at its centre. 'For those of us safely ashore, its messages from 'out there', its warnings from a dangerous peripheral world of extremes and uncertainty are reassuring.' Indeed, the more volatile the world out there is, he suggests, the more that 'home' and 'nation' are reinforced as places of safety, order, even divine protection. (Hendy, 2000: 384)

Perhaps the relationship between radio and the imagined community is of largely historical interest but there can be do doubt that in certain specific circumstances radio does have the ability to foster powerful images of belonging and identity in its listeners.

FURTHER READING

Anderson's (1983) statement of the relationship between the media and a sense of national belonging triggered the very productive use of a concept not originally developed with radio in mind. Both Douglas (1999: 22–5) and Hilmes (1997: 11–23) made use of the concept and, more recently, Hendy's history of BBC Radio 4 also stresses radio's influence on the imagination (2007: 382–9).

Intimacy

> **The sense of personal closeness or familiarity that can exist between radio (or its presenters) and listeners.**

The idea that radio is intimate is something of a commonplace in radio literature. Crisell refers to radio as 'an intimate medium' (1994: 11) and Shingler and Wieringa write about 'the unusual intimacy between radio and its audience' (1998: 114). Adopting a slightly more critical stance, Hendy acknowledges radio's 'claims to intimacy and friendliness', which may, ironically, contribute to the listener's 'sense of alienation' in the modern world (2000: 150). The intimacy claim exists for a variety of radio formats and genres but certainly includes the experience of listening to radio drama and to the companionable chat of the radio DJ.

There are various factors that contribute to the sense of intimacy. These include, first, the fact that most radio listening is an individual act; second that some radio, and especially radio drama, invites the listener to work with their imagination and so inhabit an inner world; third, that radio address is often direct; and, finally, that the radio persona adopted by presenters and DJs is often that of an ordinary and friendly person.

For some commentators there is an historical dimension to radio's intimacy, not an essential characteristic of the medium but a deliberate policy, probably the result of the threatening arrival of television:

intimacy

Exploiting the medium's ability to establish intimate relations with its audience has undoubtedly been one of the most important lessons learned by radio broadcasters since it became a mass medium and certainly since radio lost its family audience to television and found its main audience in a multitude of solitary listeners. (Shingler and Wieringa, 1998: 115)

Douglas provides a similar historical perspective, commenting on the fact that in the 1950s radio increasingly helped to structure people's days; they woke to radio, radio got them off to work, separated the morning from the afternoon and helped them go to sleep (1999: 220). This companionate intimacy was encouraged by the arrival of the transistor radio, which made radio portable both in the home and outside. This also resulted in changes to the 'repertoire of listening' as radio, and especially music radio, was used to tune into an individual's mood and so created 'more private, individualistic ways in which many were now listening' (Douglas, 1999: 221).

The radio DJ has probably exploited radio's potential for intimacy more than anyone else. From the 1950s, radio DJs 'created intimacy by moving between *you* and *me*' and so emphasised closeness and familiarity (Douglas, 1999: 230, original emphasis). They also hailed listeners in particular geographical locations ('all of you in New Jersey') as well as trying to connect with 'anyone in love' or 'any of you having a birthday today'. Studies of radio DJs show how they perform to establish this intimacy and do so using a variety of techniques. The DJ creates a radio 'persona', a specially performed personality created for radio, this can then be used to invite the audience in to the special inclusive (or perhaps exclusive) world of the show. Radio DJs use talk, familiarity and their own persona to 'simulate co-presence' or 'being together' (Montgomery, 1986: 428).

Brand and Scannell use the term 'discursive world' to describe the rule bound world created by Tony Blackburn (1991: 204). This is a **'radio world'** as I have described it elsewhere in this book and those who enter it by phoning or just listening become part of an intimate space to which they feel they belong. A feature of this process is the performance by the DJ of 'ordinariness', so that the listener feels a bond with the DJ who at the same time acts as a 'broker' with the more glamorous world of music and celebrity (Crisell, 1994: 69).

Some radio goes even further in the creation of intimacy, most notably the 'troubles talk' genre. Anna Raeburn's 1990s *Live and Direct* phone-in programme on the national British station Talk Radio is a good example. Her persona included a performance of 'ordinariness' as she projected herself as someone who was as fallible, vulnerable and world-weary as her listeners and callers (Atkinson and Moores, 2003). In her 'chats' with callers about their personal problems, Raeburn established a bond of intimacy using the full repertoire of 'para-social interaction'; in other words the characteristics of intimacy in face-to-face interaction (sincerity, attentiveness, empathy, caring) but performed over the air.

Yet another dimension of the intimate bond between the listener and radio is the nostalgic quality of some listening and especially to music. Radio stations which target older listeners with pop music from the past attempt to exploit the emotive response to hearing the sounds of a lost youth. In her research into radio nostalgia, Tacchi found that this type of listening acts as a buffer against the world:

> ... radio sound, and the nostalgic practices that it enables could be viewed as creating both a link to past or distant memories and places, and a resistance to conditions of modernity that fragment such connections, often experienced in terms of isolation or loneliness. (Tacchi, 2003: 291)

There may be many other radio genres that foster the unusually close and personal link commonly referred to as intimacy. At root it owes a lot to radio's invisibility, which results in it being experienced entirely inside the listener's head rather than objectified on the screen.

FURTHER READING

Shingler and Wieringa (1998: 114–17) provide a useful starting point for further reading. Douglas (1999: 229–33) discusses the intimacy encouraged by the performance of the early radio DJs. The analysis of Anna Raeburn's performance of intimacy in therapy radio is intriguing (Atkinson and Moores, 2003).

Liveness

> *The quality of most radio output that conveys a sense of being live, whether or not it actually is.*

One of the defining features of radio is its sense of being live. The large majority of contemporary radio is live: it is broadcast very nearly at the moment that we hear it. This is true of a large proportion of music radio (but probably less than most people think) and most news and sport, together with a great deal of talk radio and almost all phone-in shows. The exceptions are those speech programmes which are pre-recorded and 'crafted' in the process of recording and editing and other post-production (see the entry on **Recording**). This is clearly true of almost all drama and all documentaries and features. In addition even in *apparently* live programmes there may be pre-recorded inserts, even if they appear to be live. An interview with a busy politician may have been pre-recorded even if we are given the impression that, is live: that is to say it is 'as live' or conveys the impression of 'liveness'.

In the early years of radio, and indeed in the first decades of television, all programmes were live. Recording technology was so cumbersome that it was used only if it was really essential. In the US some pre-war programmes had to be recorded because of the different time zones and in the UK some programmes were recorded to be sent to countries in the Empire or, in the case of pre-war commercial radio, recorded in London prior to being sent to Europe for broadcast (Street, 2006a: 103). But the large majority of BBC radio was live and that continued to be the case until the introduction of the tape recorder in the 1950s.

In his influential discussion of liveness on television, Ellis makes the point that its live quality was extremely important, 'live performance gave television a direct and intimate link with its audience, and this link became one of the defining characteristics of broadcast television' (2000: 31). His comments about television and its apparent liveness are also pertinent for radio. Even when programmes have been pre-recorded, a great deal of effort goes into creating the illusion that they are live. So, for example, the use of direct address ('I', 'you') adds to the sense of 'now', to the 'rhetoric of liveness'. The presenter might also greet the audience ('hello', 'good evening', 'welcome') as if the programme is live and also use temporal markers like 'coming up', 'later' and 'come back after the break'. The sense of liveness, that the broadcast (both television and radio) was live and that what the audience saw and heard was actually happening at that moment went hand-in-hand with the experience of **co-presence**. So, for example, watching the extremely popular Saturday evening ITV light entertainment show *Blind Date* the audience was encouraged to believe not only that the programme was live (it wasn't) but also that they shared the experience with millions of others in a sort of mini television event (Ellis, 2000: 34).

Turning to radio we can see an equal effort to make the pre-recorded programme appear live. Recent developments in technology and in the economics of radio production have led to an increase in pre-recorded

DJ speech on commercial radio stations. Why pay an expensive DJ to come into a studio early on a wet morning when he or she could just as well record all of their links from a nearby studio, or at home, at a time that suits them, and send them in over an ISDN line? The phenomenon of 'voice tracking' refers to pre-recorded links for later transmission, often using a special music playout software (Starkey, 2004a: 248). There are clearly some dangers with this:

> Practically, if used without regulatory control, at the extremes automation could enable a whole radio station to broadcast without any presenters or technical operators at all, or to appear to have the same presenter broadcasting 24 hours a day. While non-stop music sequences have always been an option, common sense would suggest that listeners might quickly rumble the presenter who appears to be permanently 'on air' and never sleep.
> (Starkey, 2004a: 100)

The quality of liveness is communicated largely through the medium of speech. Tolson argues that there are three key components of 'media talk' (or what Scannell calls 'broadcast talk') and these are interactivity, performativity (the performance of the presenter) and what he calls 'liveliness' (2006: 9). Liveliness possesses the same qualities as liveness in that it gives the impression of unscripted speech, which has an unpredictable and spontaneous quality and is delivered to an audience co-present in time. In radio there are a number of devices that can be used to enhance this sense of here-and-now spontaneity. Because we know that most sport is not pre-recorded there is some guarantee that it is actually live. This clearly adds to the sense of unpredictability mentioned by Tolson. Will the team win? Will the golf ball go in the hole? It also guarantees the relative spontaneity and excitement of the commentator's speech. So most radio sport is live and also has that special quality of liveness. The radio **phone-in**, one of the great success stories of contemporary radio, is also based on the assumption that it is live. The fact that we are invited to phone in certainly appears to be a guarantee that the broadcast is happening now. The general liveness of the phone-in is enhanced by the clearly unscripted speech of the contributors and the apparently spontaneous attempts of the presenters to deal with them.

In a sense liveness is both an illusion, an artificially created sense of spontaneity and being here and now, but also a reflection of the fact that the radio broadcaster exists in the same temporal world that we do. Not only the time of day but also the same point in the week and in the year.

liveness

Hendy refers to the way that 'radio's *temporal rhythms* – its narrative structures, hourly cycles and daily and weekly schedules – connect with the temporal rhythms of our everyday lives' (2000: 178, original emphasis). He refers to Garner's enigmatic claim that the real 'text' of radio is the 'clock on the studio wall'. That, in other words, the content of much live radio is simply a constant affirmation of what the time is. Radio's strongly temporal quality, reflecting the moment in the day with a breakfast show or an afternoon play or late night phone-in all contributes to the quality of liveness. The programme may have been pre-recorded but that is disguised in the attempt to convince the listener that what they hear is going out live and is temporally co-present.

So why is all of this effort made to insist on the liveness of radio? Furthermore, why does it matter for an understanding of radio? If we return to Tolson's attempt to define the characteristics or 'key concepts' of media talk we find a useful list for understanding how radio itself succeeds in holding its audience – in keeping people listening despite the considerable temptations of other media. This list can be adapted and developed to include other concepts that are discussed elsewhere in this book. Radio is often described as an **intimate** medium and one that fosters a simulated **co-presence** with its listeners. A friend that is also somehow in the same place as the listener. Liveness is a critically important part of this effect. The rhetoric of liveness (spontaneity, lack of script) contributes both to radio's intimacy but also to co-presence. These three qualities are at the core of what radio is. What is striking is that they are not present in the personalised form of 'radio' or audio and most importantly the podcast. On-demand audio would struggle to give the listener that same sense of intimacy, co-presence and liveness that is definitive of contemporary radio. Herein lies a clue to why studio based live radio has so far managed to survive the threat of personalised media. What you hear on the radio may not be the music or speech which you would necessarily choose but at least it feels 'now' – at least you feel connected to a person and others co-existing at one moment in time.

FURTHER READING

One of the original statements about the importance of liveness concerns television, but is revealing for radio as well (Ellis, 2000). Starkey (2004a) explains how technology is used to create the impression of liveness and Tolson (2006: 11–14) contrasts liveness with what he calls 'liveliness'.

Noise

Noise is one of the codes of radio and refers to sound content that is not speech, music or silence. Noise is created either naturally, accidentally or artificially, as in a sound effect.

Crisell has claimed that speech is the primary code of radio (1994: 3), (see the entry on **Codes**). That is to say that speech is the principal means of communication as, arguably, the visual image is on television. Crisell could be challenged by saying that **music** is radio's primary code. In the great expanse of music radio it is the music which is communicating and the speech of the DJ is entirely secondary. Whichever of these arguments is correct there are in addition the sounds that accompany speech and music and add to the meaning of radio in sometimes quite subtle and unacknowledged ways. If we see these as constituting a further code of radio then silence itself should be added as the final code.

The non-speech, non-music noises of radio include natural incidental sounds as well as those that are artificially created, normally for use in radio drama. Sound effects are often an important part of radio drama and the success or otherwise of sound effects depends on what they signify to the listener. One way to think about this is as a sonic shorthand; the creaking of ropes signifies being on a boat, the seagull's cry signifies the seaside, the police siren means the city and birdsong means the countryside (Shingler and Wieringa, 1998: 146). As suggested in the entry on the **Soundscape** the sound environment is full of these potential signifiers that can be used in radio production to create a sense of place.

The presence of noise, including artificially created effects as well as natural noise, can be important in other radio genres. In sports commentaries the sound of the crowd is of critical importance to signify the excitement of the live crowd. The crowd's roar, cheers, whistles, shouts and so on all add to the commentary and provide a very obvious additional form of non-verbal commentary on the reaction of the crowd. In news radio, sound can also play an important part, this is particularly so when a reporter is at the scene and the soundscape is an important part of the story. Here is an example from a report on riots in Britain in the 1980s:

> SHOUTING AND BEATING OF BATONS ON SHIELDS. The noise that you can hear now is the police beating on their riot shields as they move into a barrier in the centre of the road. They are coming under fire now. Missiles. There's a large crowd of youngsters at the other end of the street. …
>
> The stones really are flying in. Some of the youths, their faces hidden by scarves and masks. … (a) car that was taken has been crashed into some railings and the police are now moving in again, beating their riot shields and trying to break up a crowd of youths who are now sprinting back up the street, sill throwing bottles and bricks at the police … SHOUTING, CRIES AND SMASHING GLASS. (Crook, 1998: 276)

Here the dramatic sounds of the riot and the police response are almost as important as the words of the reporter. Similarly a report from a war is given added meaning by the sounds of explosions and gunfire.

In her account of talk radio in the USA, Douglas comments on the often creative use of sound by 'shock jocks' like Don Imus and Howard Stern:

> … both of whom had ensemble casts of characters supporting them, used sound effects (not the least of which are those which are produced by the human mouth), voice impersonations, sometimes graphic descriptions of what was going on in the studio, and uncontrolled giggling and laughter to convey a clubby atmosphere of fun. (1999: 286)

In addition, the pioneer talk radio host Rush Limbaugh has been known to use the sound of a vacuum cleaner in the studio when discussing abortion. The vacuum sounds acting as an unpleasant, and politically charged, reminder of the medical procedure itself.

Noise is at times significant for the communication of meaning on radio and yet it is all too easily forgotten in discussions of other radio codes.

FURTHER READING

Shingler and Wieringa (1998: 51–61) provide a very readable and comprehensive introduction to the subject of noise. Crisell (1994: 44–8) discusses what he calls 'sounds' in the context of the codes of radio.

Radiogenic

The word radiogenic is a contested term in radio studies but has been used to describe subjects or content particularly suited to a non-visual medium.

The term photogenic refers to something that is suited to the medium of photography; it makes a good photograph. Some people and some places, to take just two examples, seem to lend themselves to being photographed. The term radiogenic may be much harder to define but it has been used in the BBC for almost 25 years 'to describe programmes made specifically for the medium of radio, utilising to the maximum its distinctive qualities' (Everett, 1999). At the most basic level we might describe something as radiogenic if it is particularly suited to the radio medium.

In the late 1990s, a group of British academics held an online discussion about the term and its precise meaning. Some thought it meant 'having its origins in radio', or designed specifically with radio in mind. This would exclude music that, although very suited to radio, does not have its origins in radio broadcasting. A different point of view, suggested by Tim Wall (1999), is that radiogenic means following the conventional aesthetic of radio. This is a useful idea because it challenges the notion that there is something 'essentially' radio-like about a piece of drama, for example. The problem with that idea is that radio, like photography, cannot be distilled to some sort of pure essence, it follows changing conventions which are themselves the product of global and national radio culture. Wall comments on what the radio convention might be 'since the 1960s it is a convention based upon the playing of music' (1999) It is certainly true that music radio has become a dominant, if not *the* dominant, form. It could be argued that it is music and not speech that is the primary code of radio and therefore what makes good radio, what is radiogenic, is music-based (see entry on **Codes**). In addition, the non-visual nature of music (and to a large extent the non-visual quality of DJ talk) lends itself to radio as opposed to other media.

radiogenic

93

There is clearly considerable disagreement about the meaning of the term radiogenic in academia, but there can be little doubt that at a more practical level the term is extremely useful for the analysis of radio. If we assume that music does count as radiogenic we can add some other examples. In radio drama it is possible to hear the thoughts of the character through the use of the interior monologue. So thoughts and psychological state are potentially 'radiogenic'. The sounds around us, our sonic environment, or the 'soundscape', is also radiogenic. Uncluttered by visual images we can hear these sounds more completely because they are on radio. The accents of people are also radiogenic, as are the stories that people tell about themselves in their own voices. Two striking examples of radiogenic story telling, one fact and one fiction, appear in Hendy's history of BBC Radio 4. The BBC presenter Glyn Worsnip was diagnosed with a degenerative brain disease. In the programme *A Lone Voice* (1988) he told the 'full, ghastly truth' of his decline. *Spoonface Steinberg* (1998) was in some ways a similar exploration of decline and tragedy. It was a radio play which told the story of a young girl keeping a radio diary as she dies from cancer (Hendy, 2007: 378–9). Both are examples of radiogenic subjects that almost certainly worked better on radio than they would have done on television.

Politics and the coverage of politics in current affairs programmes could also be called radiogenic. Uncluttered by pictures of politicians and unnecessary visual images, radio can focus on the political arguments and evidence. Similarly, intellectual ideas, philosophical debate, work better without pictures and so are radiogenic as the highly successful BBC Radio 4 series *In Our Time*, which often consists of three academics discussing scientific and philosophical ideas, has shown. While we are on the subject of politics, President Franklin D. Roosevelt's *Fireside Chats* were also surely radiogenic. Roosevelt was a great radio performer with a voice suited to radio and his intimate style of address, which he used to talk to the electorate about the problems of the depression and the Second World War, may have been a success because it was on radio.

FURTHER READING

Unfortunately there is no published discussion of the meaning and significance of this concept. There is, however, an intriguing early discussion on the Radio Studies email list (http://www.jiscmail.ac.uk) where the comments of Everett and Wall are particularly useful.

Radio World

The radio world refers to the discursive space (or imaginary world) created and ruled over by the presenter and into which callers are invited to enter.

This entry translates the concept of the 'discursive space' (or 'discursive world') into the slightly more transparent 'radio world'. The idea that the presenter of some radio programmes creates an imaginary world with its own boundaries and rules, centred around the persona of the presenter, is an interesting and useful idea and one which is given rather more emphasis by this retitling.

In almost every case the radio world exists in the radio studio and is controlled by the presenter. The best examples of this are to be found in American talk radio and in music radio. In both cases, phone-ins are used to involve listeners and this makes it possible for members of the audience to enter the radio world.

Probably the best account of this phenomenon is found in an analysis of the *Tony Blackburn Show* (Brand and Scannell, 1991). Blackburn was one of the earliest music radio DJs on the BBC and developed a particularly complex and idiosyncratic radio persona, most notably on Radio London from 1984 to 1989. Blackburn's radio world was ruled by his persona; a construct which included Blackburn as miserable divorcee, as sex-obsessed male, as prankster and fun-lover, and as an anti-authority troublemaker. Those who called in to speak to 'the leader' or 'the living legend' had to understand and obey the rules of his 'discursive kingdom' or radio world. Those who did not were swiftly removed.

Another good example centres on the figure of a much more recent BBC Radio 1 DJ Chris Evans. Tolson provides a revealing account of the way callers enter into Evans' world. In this case the caller is Amanda:

> It is a world where anyone can enter the media and, like Amanda, have their fifteen seconds of fame. It is a world where ordinary people interact with media personnel, and, by extension, the mediated community of mini-celebrity which they inhabit. (2006: 129)

radio world

95

Once again it is the persona of the DJ that is at the centre of the radio world, embodying and expressing the values of the programme. Evans' world is a daily soap opera acted out by his co-presenters and production staff with him in the studio in a 'zoo radio' format. At one level it is very mundane, full of references to eating biscuits and having a chat. It is also adolescent and a world which frequently transgresses the boundaries of taste.

Another BBC radio DJ, John Peel, also established a unique and unusual world on his speech programme, *Home Truths*. This was a largely pre-recorded one-hour magazine programme and that gave Peel much greater control over listener contributions. He adopted a particularly eccentric and entertaining persona of an ageing family man, out of touch with the modern world around him. Contributors were invited to send in recorded contributions which, of course, had to be synchronous with the programme's and Peel's values. Eccentricity, family life (problems of), national identity, ageing, all were acceptable themes. Although Peel described the programme itself as wildly eclectic it was in fact an exercise in quite strict discursive conformism (Chignell and Devlin, 2007).

The concept of the discursive space or radio world is a useful reminder of the institutional and artificial nature of interaction and talk on live radio. Tolson refers to it as 'para-social interaction', not real but something that happens over a distance and is largely imagined. The rhetoric or illusion of the phone-in is that it is a spontaneous and authentic exchange between the presenter and whoever calls in. The reality is that the caller is entering into a highly controlled rule-bound environment. The radio world acts to reinforce and bolster the persona of the DJ or presenter because it is created in their image, but it also reinforces the interactive and participatory nature of the programme and a sense of a community of listeners united by their acceptance of the set rules and values.

FURTHER READING

The definitive account of this concept is Brand and Scannell (1991) on the *Tony Blackburn Show*. For a more contemporary (if derivative) usage see Chignell and Devlin (2007) on John Peel.

Reception

A term used to describe both the experience of listening and the technology of the radio receiver or set.

This entry is concerned with the technological aspect of reception and the development of the radio receiver, formerly known as the radio set. In the early 1920s, radio receivers were often made by enthusiastic amateurs (also known as 'hams' or 'DXers'). Using kits or simple instructions, they built crystal sets in which a fine wire (a 'cat's whisker') was manipulated while touching a mineral crystal. The sounds picked up were listened to using headphones. The 'valve' or 'tube' radio was a larger item powered by heavy and very messy wet batteries; also listened to using headphones. The first plug-in radio, which removed the need for batteries, was sold in 1927 and gradually loudspeakers replaced headphones. To make early sets attractive in the home the design increasingly resembled a piece of furniture. Well designed (but large and heavy) radio sets sat in the corners of sitting rooms or perched on the table in the kitchen. Some 1930s radios reflected modernist designs; the Pye 'rising sun' grill and Ekco bakelite cabinets (bakelite was an early form of plastic) were both bold and modern. The pre-war radio set was very much a family item, often listened to by the family as a group. In an attempt to attract women listeners, in 1931 Ekco introduced the first receiver with a full range of station names printed on the dial; the belief being that until then men were using their presumed technical skills to be in control of the radio set (Taylor-McCain, 2007). There were portable radios as well using improved batteries and these were particularly popular in Britain where the electricity supply in the 1930s was often unreliable. Car radios were introduced in 1930 in America but were too expensive to be anything other than a luxury.

Post-war there was a revolution in the radio receiver. The transistor was invented in 1947 but it was not until 1954 that Texas Instruments (TI) developed the first pocket sized transistor radio (Ellis, 2004: 1413). This prototype was sent to American radio manufacturers but not a single one responded to TI's follow-up inquiries. Eventually the first transistor radio was made and put on the market by an Indiana company in November 1954. Adoption of the new technology was slow despite the fact that the transistor in comparison with the valve or tube was cheaper, smaller, lighter, longer lasting, more durable and used less power. In post-war America, consumers wanted to put the years of austerity behind them and buy large cars and other consumer items; size mattered.

In her cultural history of radio in America, Douglas (1999) pays particular attention to technological change. For her, the transistor played an integral part in the formation of youth culture from the late 1950s. To begin with it helped take radio listening out of the home:

> At work, in the car, on the beach, people – especially the young – brought radio with them and used it to stake out their social space by blanketing a particular area with their music, their sportscasts, their announcers. With transistors, sound defined social space. (Douglas, 1999: 221)

As radio increasingly became the place to hear the latest cool DJs with their black inspired music and slang, the transistor offered the chance of 'breakout listening', 'a conscious turn away from mainstream, adult, white culture and an eager, often defiant entrance into an auditory realm in which a fairly new species – the teenager – was welcomed, embraced and flattered' (Douglas, 1999: 222). Where previously the family had clustered around the tube or valve radio set to listen to an older generation of comics and singers, now listening was something done in the bedroom or with friends. There was, as a result, a huge increase in transistor sales in the 1960s in both the USA and the UK and this expansion in sales was greatly assisted by the new cheaper models imported from Japan and Hong Kong.

Today, in the UK, there is a bewildering variety of radio receivers. The cheap, portable FM/AM transistor remains dominant, there may be as many as a hundred million in British homes. The digital radio (DAB) experiment in the UK is still very much in its infancy (see the entry on **Transmission**). Although digital radio in the UK can be listened to on digital television sets and on the Internet its success will partly depend on the sale of easy-to-use digital radio sets. Early DAB receivers were eerily reminiscent of the valve radios of the last century; heavy, expensive, non-portable and even designed to mimic the classic sets of the past (as in the case of Pure Digital's Pure Evoke range). Because DAB is not a global technology manufacturers do not benefit from the economies of scale which have driven down the price of other consumer technologies and the cheapest DAB sets, at the time of writing, remain five times more expensive than the cheapest AM/FM transistor radios. It remains to be seen whether DAB will prove to be a successful technology and the DAB receiver as popular as its predecessors.

The extraordinary success of the mobile or cell phone around the world suggests a way forward for the kind of cheap, portable, ubiquitous radio described in Douglas's account of the transistor in the 1960s. Indeed Bull's (2005) account of that other form of personalised media, the iPod®, is strongly reminiscent of Douglas writing about the transistor; both serving to carve out a social and cultural space for their listeners.

FURTHER READING

There are excellent summaries of the technology in Sterling (2004a); see especially Ellis, S. (2004) on transistor radios and Sterling (2004c) on earlier receivers. There is a highly readable, and probably definitive, account of the rise of the transistor radio in the USA in Douglas (1999: 219–55).

Secondariness

> *A term used to describe the way that radio is either secondary to television or, more usually, that radio listening is secondary to some other activity.*

Radio is often referred to as a 'secondary' medium. There are two related interpretations of this. The first meaning is that radio is less important than the primary medium of television. Second, the term can imply that because listening to the radio is secondary, or ancillary, to another activity, it creates a sonic background for our lives. Hilmes discusses these two interpretations in her answer to the question she posed herself, 'what happened to radio?' (Hilmes and Loviglio, 2002: 1). Once upon a time radio was central to people's lives and, in the USA, it was the most important cultural institution during the turbulent decades from the 1920s to the 1960s. It played the central role in socialising the population and in the creation of an American identity. Then along came television and radio slipped in importance to become 'secondary' in two senses:

> After television usurped much of [radio's primary] role, radio became the background sound of our lives, our most persistent and ubiquitous media companion, losing the main spotlight of prime time in the living room but keeping us company during the rest of the day in our kitchens, bedroom, bathrooms, automobiles, offices, and workshops; serenading us while we walked and jogged; filling us in on local and national news, sports reports and play-by-play, weather, school closings, and emergency bulletins; and generally serving us as a vital, though ancillary, component of our informational and entertainment universe. (Hilmes and Loviglio, 2002: 1)

Here, radio is seen as the trusty companion to people's lives without ever being the main guest at the media party, a place taken by television and, arguably, then usurped by the Internet.

This was certainly not the vision of the radio pioneers and especially not in the case of the BBC. The pages of BBC publications of the early 1930s are full of advice and censure on the subject of how to listen. Once radio became a permanent feature of the domestic space, often partly disguised as a heavy piece of furniture, radio listening was a largely social activity. In their history of the BBC in the 1930s, Scannell and Cardiff describe how listeners were told not to 'listen with half an ear' and to either concentrate on the radio or switch it off (1991: 370). Listeners were encouraged to choose programmes from the listings in the same way that a borrower would choose a book from a library. This was listening 'by appointment' and in the case of some of the BBC's demanding and culturally uplifting talks and drama such commitment would have been essential.

In the UK, the Second World War had a radical impact on radio. There was a much greater awareness of the audience, encouraged by the start of audience research in the late 1930s. Workers in the munitions factories could listen to *Music While You Work*, a good early example of radio as background. Another wartime development in the BBC which acknowledged that people did other things while they listened to the radio was the introduction of the magazine format (see the entry on the

Magazine). *The Kitchen Front* was a radio magazine, in other words it was divided up into short talk sequences and features (about cooking for the family, a celebrity interview, listeners' letters, a comedy sketch) aimed at meeting the needs of women in the home who were also occupied with domestic chores.

Television became the dominant medium in Britain in the early 1950s and a few years earlier in the USA. Television took audiences, money and the best performers from radio. But radio had a small technological trick up its sleeve. The transistor was invented in 1947 and the lightweight, highly portable and cheap transistor radio created a flexible companion (see the entry on **Reception**). Radios, increasingly tuned to the new VHF (or FM) wavebands and playing top 40 hits, were now in cars, bedrooms, kitchens, garages and on the beach. And so radio, while certainly becoming less culturally important and losing a substantial part of its evening audience to television, became a ubiquitous source of sound companionship and information. The result of this transformation was to replace listening to specific programmes with the less attentive phenomenon of hearing. Radio stations learned to reflect the rhythms of daily life and encourage listening to stations over a period of time. Upcoming events in the radio day are sign-posted ('coming up soon ...', 'on the hour ...') to keep the audience tuned to that station. This passive and inattentive audience may also be more vulnerable to advertising as its critical defences are down (Hendy, 2000: 182).

The phenomenon of 'drive time' illustrates radio's secondariness particularly well. The first radio sets were fitted in cars in America in the 1930s and, by 1953, nearly 60 per cent of automobiles were equipped with car radios (Rothenbuhler and McCourt, 2002: 378). The radio industry responded by creating drive time shows that were explicitly designed for an audience for whom listening was a secondary activity. Drive time is now one of the most popular slots in the radio day and in the USA this is true for both commercial radio and National Public Radio (NPR).

More recently the advent of the Internet has created another opportunity for listening while doing something else. Radio can be an excellent accompaniment to surfing the net. Indeed, the phenomenon of the Internet radio station acknowledges this and being online gives the Internet user a huge variety of stations to listen to.

It would be wrong to accept uncritically radio's new position as a secondary medium. There are clearly moments on radio that demand our attention and get it. A brilliant DJ making us laugh or a news item which makes us stop what we are doing; public service radio news analysis or a well scripted drama will have an audience of listeners who concentrate on that output. It could also be argued that the cook making tonight's dinner while listening to the radio is *primarily* a radio listener and peeling the potatoes is the secondary activity. Referring to the other sense of radio's secondariness, to television, in both the USA and the UK radio has been politically very influential in recent years. American talk radio in the 1990s made a major contribution to the groundswell of support for conservative republicanism and voting behaviour. In the UK, BBC Radio 4's *Today* remains the most influential political programme across radio and television. It was no surprise that the resignation of Greg Dyke, the BBC's Director General in 2004, was the result of accusations made in the lead up to the Iraq War not on BBC television but on *Today*. Indeed, the quality of radio news and analysis, especially on public service radio, is one of the most important reasons for radio's survival. To this can be added the unprecedented extent of popular opinion aired through the use of the phone-ins on both sides of the Atlantic. Radio may sometimes deserve the label 'secondary' but it is frequently the primary medium for the coverage of political news and opinions. For many people radio continues to be the most reliable source of information and arguably, at times, the primary source for the expression of diverse opinions and informed comment.

FURTHER READING

For an early statement about radio's secondariness see Crisell (1994: x–xi). Hilmes provides perhaps the most authoritative statement (Hilmes and Loviglio, 2002: 1–19) and the chapter in the same book by Rothenbuhler and McCourt (2002) is illuminating.

Sound Culture

> *The sound culture is the auditory environment (or soundscape) located within its wider social and cultural context.*

The entry **Soundscape** discusses the concept with its connotation of a sonic landscape or environment. It is suggested in that entry that this was a useful idea in radio studies because it describes the meaningful sonic environment (the rumble of traffic, the music coming out of a shop, the distant police siren – all evocative of urban living), which is frequently present in radio output and which, on occasions, includes the sound of radio itself. The concept of a sound culture (also called an auditory or aural culture) is directly connected to the soundscape, indeed the distinction between the two is not that clear cut. In a sense the sound culture is the bigger picture, it requires us to step back and ask questions about the origins and nature of the soundscape; why does it sound as it does? What are the broader social and cultural influences on what we hear in our everyday lives?

Social and cultural organisation are largely responsible for the sound landscape that we inhabit and these inevitably change over time. In the pre-industrial European world one of the defining features of the soundscape was the tolling of the church bell. It told the workers in the field of the progress of their day's toil but was also an auditory marker of the community briefly enveloped in the sound of the bell. It also reminded those who heard it of the centrality of the church in their lives. The bell's ring was part of the soundscape but the social and religious dimensions, which add meaning to the sound, are also part of the wider sound culture.

Industrialisation created a very different soundscape, the soundscape of modernity (Thompson, 2004). The cities became unprecedentedly loud; 'the din of modern technology: the roar of elevated trains, the rumble of internal combustion engines, the crackle and hiss of radio transmissions' (Thompson, 2004: 6). Faced with this often alienating din the science of acoustics was born as 20th-century city dwellers strove to create a quieter world and even to eliminate unwanted sound. Part of the aural mix in the USA was the sound of jazz, which came to represent the American city itself (as it does to this day in the soundtracks of Hollywood). Jazz was closely related to urban noise and the noise of the ghetto described here as it came up a Harlem ventilation shaft by the jazz musician Duke Ellington:

> You get the full essence of Harlem in an air shaft. You hear fights, you smell dinner, you hear people making love. You hear intimate gossip floating down. You hear the radio. An air shaft is one great big loudspeaker. (Quoted in Thompson, 1994: 131)

These sounds, including jazz, were part of the particularly rich and complex sound culture of America's African population living in the ghettos. A soundscape that was socially, historically and culturally determined as was the often racist reaction to it. Jazz was seen as the music of the jungle capable of driving people to 'the vilest deeds'. This was 'nigger music' and 'whorehouse music' and no wonder so much effort was expended in keeping it off the airwaves (Hilmes, 1997: 49).

The contemporary urban soundscape has a uniquely electronic quality:

> The *chkty-chkty-chkty-chkty* spilling out of someone else's headphones, the *yeow-yeow* clearing the way for ambulances and police cars, the *bllliiiiii* heralding the banalaties of a stranger's one-sided conversation on a mobile phone – these serve as a keen reminders that most of us live immersed in a world of sound. (Smith, 2003: 127)

So much of contemporary sound culture is the sound of electronic media; the personalised media of the phone and the iPod®. Music, the radio and television at home, recorded sound in the shops, pub and nightclub. In cultural terms this soundscape has to be seen as a highly commercialised and global environment in which what we hear is determined by the boardrooms of the media conglomerates. This is a soundscape largely detached from and ignorant of the local environment. In this global, commercialised soundscape, radio is highly complicit, except perhaps where it dares to challenge sterile, homogenised and formatted programming (Douglas, 1999: 356).

It would be quite reasonable to ask whether the concept of the sound culture is relevant to radio. The answer is surely that sound itself, and our knowledge of the world through sound, is fundamental to radio. Crisell has been much castigated for referring to the '**blindness**' of radio, but he was surely right to emphasise the bald fact that the medium is all about sound. For students and scholars of radio this necessitates an acknowledgement of the importance of sound as a subject in addition to radio and this means that the critical 'thinking with our ears' advocated by Bull and Back (2003: 2) is not something we can ignore. If we can see radio in its broadcasting and media context as well as in the context of the sound culture our understanding will be more complete.

FURTHER READING

This is not an easy concept to pin down but for further reading try Bull and Back's (2003: 1–17) introductory chapter. For an historical perspective, very important here, see Thompson (1994) or Hilmes (1997).

Soundscape

> *The soundscape is the sound (or sonic) environment: both as we hear it in our daily lives and as it is heard on radio.*

The Canadian composer R. Murray Shafer first coined this useful term to refer to the 'sonic environment' (Bull and Back, 2003: 21). A soundscape is like a landscape but instead of the physical and therefore visual features of geography a sound landscape consists of all the sounds in an environment (see the previous entry on **Sound Culture**). An urban soundscape will today often be dominated by the sound of cars, a police siren, a noisy air-conditioning system, the anonymous crashes and thumps of machinery. This contrasts with historical soundscapes, which we obviously cannot hear but which can be at least guessed at with a bit of detective work. The soundscape in the fields outside a small market town in England 300 years ago might include the talk of people at work, singing, dogs barking, the rasps, swishes, cuts and thumps of tools and perhaps the noise of a hunt; horn blasts, men shouting and galloping horses (Smith, 2003: 133). In the context of radio it is useful to make a distinction between the natural sonic environment in which we live our lives and the specific 'radio soundscape' which we hear on radio. The latter has been selected by the producer or presenter. This radio soundscape could be used to describe radio drama or other radio with significant levels of actuality (a football match or the sound of battle in a war report).

In radio production work, and especially pre-recorded documentaries, the producer may want to capture the soundscape by making a 'wild track' recording. This is a recording of the sound of the environment (also called 'actuality') independent of the voice of the presenter. The soundscape in radio, however, is more than just background noise, it is itself the bearer of meanings. The sound of the seagull suggests the sea, holidays and even pleasure: 'like a landscape, a soundscape is simultaneously a physical environment and a way of perceiving that environment; it is both a world and a culture constructed to make sense of that world' (Thompson, 2004: 1).

In her analysis of radio soundscapes, Frances Gray discusses the radio play. She stresses the act of imagination in listening: 'it is not only a question of imaginatively constructing characters and setting, but of assuming the active role of a listener in a soundscape where the fictional interacts and comments on the real' (2004, 257). So the listener is at the heart of a soundscape, a point of intersection between the sound environment and their own imagination.

One of the most important developments in the urban soundscape, in 'the soundscape of modernity', was the invention of electroacoustic devices in the last century; including telephones, gramophones, film and radio itself. So radio is a creator of radio soundscapes, but is also a very important part of our own domestic sonic environment. The social anthropologist Tacchi looked at the conflict between a husband and wife over the choice of radio station. Faye liked pop music but Bob was a fanatical BBC Radio 4 listener and forced Faye to listen too (Tacchi, 2000: 158). Tacchi describes how Bob 'inflicted his soundscape' on his wife in a battle reminiscent of the family rows over a teenager's music blaring from a bedroom, redolent of teen rebellion and defiance. Here radio is seen as an important and meaning-laden part of the domestic soundscape, even contributing to the identity of the person who chose that particular station.

An understanding of soundscapes requires us to step outside the limitations of radio and to acknowledge the wider sonic environment of which radio itself can be a part. The contemporary urban soundscape features the sounds of the mobile phone, its ring, the one-sided conversation we overhear and the muffled music on someone else's iPod®. As radio becomes more portable and a greater part of the personalised mobile environment, it re-enters the public soundscape which, in the form of the 1960s transistor radio playing top 40 hits, it once occupied.

FURTHER READING

R. Murray Shafer (2003) provides an early and very influential account and is an obvious starting point for further reading. A selective look at Thompson (2004) would be very worthwhile. A highly readable and interesting use of the concept is provided by Gray (2004).

soundscape

Part III
The Radio
Industry

Advertising

Advertising on radio involves the sale of airtime to businesses to allow them to sell their products, usually as short 'spot' advertisements or in the form of programme sponsorship.

Who pays for radio? The listener pays for the radio set or receiver but only rarely for the radio service, the programmes themselves. Globally, radio broadcasting is paid for in a variety of ways including direct state funding, indirect state funding (in the case of the BBC through the licence fee; a form of indirect taxation), by the support of a charitable or non-government organisation (as in the case of much of the community radio in Africa), by direct subscription (for example the US satellite services Sirius and XM) but above all through the sale of airtime for advertising.

The history of radio advertising goes back to the beginning of radio itself, in fact, as Hilmes points out, the histories of radio and of the radio advertising agencies run parallel to each other (1997: 114). Although there is some disagreement about what the very first radio advertisement was, some claim this title for a 15-minute commercial message by the real estate company Queensboro Corporation on WEAF (New York) in August 1922. Pre-war American radio advertising included both programme sponsorship and the short messages called 'spots', often grouped together into a set or block of adverts. Programme sponsorship in pre-war American radio featured shows such as the wonderfully titled *Cliquot Club Eskimos* (advertising Cliquot Club ginger ale) and the National Carbon Company's *Eveready Hour* (for other examples see the entry on **Commercialism**). The pioneering radio soap *Clara, Lu and Em* was sponsored by Super Suds in 1931 (hence the term 'soap') and then by Colgate in 1932 and Palmolive in 1935.

In this pre-war period, in both the USA and the UK, radio advertising agencies produced their own programmes. In America, for example, N.W. Ayer had a radio production department from 1923, which made dramas, literary adaptations and variety shows (Hilmes, 197: 114). In Britain, commercial radio was available only from stations in Europe.

advertising

Radios Luxembourg and Normandy were supplied with programmes by the giant advertising agency J. Walter Thompson (JWT) (Street, 2006a: 103). One of the problems of this reliance on external production was a worrying tend towards what was felt to be a deterioration in radio standards accompanied by a lack of control on the part of stations and networks over programme content. JWT quickly saw the potential of radio to connect with the needs of the mass audience:

> By 1927, JWT had recognized not only the existence but the value of 'these vast new layers of people who have money to spend and who have very few media to reach them excepting the tabloids and confession magazines' and had begun to advocate a new 'lowbrow' approach to advertising. (JWT internal document, quoted in Hilmes, 1997: 117)

The JWT heritage in Britain is tinged with rather more affection and nostalgia. A generation of listeners remembered the Horlicks-sponsored Sunday evening show on Radio Luxembourg, *The League of Ovaltineys*, which 'achieved immortality through what might legitimately be called the most successful advertising jingle of all time' (Street, 2006a: 12). The jingle started with the words 'we are the Ovaltineys' and finished 'because we all drink Ovaltine we're happy girls and boys'.

Radio advertising represents something of a mixed blessing for the radio industry. On the one hand, it brings in very large amounts of money not easily available from another source. In 2002, radio advertising revenue in the USA was a staggering US$19.5b. But the money comes at a price. Radio advertising can intrude on radio programming and can have a negative effect. The historical examples cited above illustrate this well. In America, the influence of the agencies in the 1920s contributed to a perceived decline in standards and control. The agencies were somehow more in tune with the 'vulgarities' of modern consumerism than the broadcasters:

> A profound social upheaval was underway in the 1920s ... Victorian standards of taste, personal conduct, and morality were disintegrating. The temper of the times favoured radio's commercial trend ... The advertising men, more conscious of the trend than the network executives, took advantage of the jazzed-up tempo of the age. Almost before the broadcasters knew what had happened, the advertising agencies took over – and it was they who set the tone. (Sydney Head, quoted in Street, 2006a: 85)

The unwanted influence of radio advertising is of course still seen today. Audience research on the attitudes of British listeners to commercial radio show that although they accept the inevitability of adverts they think there are too many of them and that they cut into their enjoyment of a programme (Ofcom, 2004: 42). On the other hand, as in the case of the much loved Ovaltineys, a sponsors message can be fun and popular.

Any evaluation of the impact of advertising on radio has to take into account a variety of factors and issues. On the negative side, advertisers may exert an unwanted influence as a result of their demand for a certain slice of the audience demographic. This can push radio into restricted formats and generally pander to the lowest common denominator of safe and predictable radio; hence the dominance of contemporary hits and country formats in the USA. Radio is also victim to the extremely unreliable nature of radio advertising revenue. Any down-turn in the economy seems to impact badly on radio advertising first. And radio adverts can just be an irritating distraction in radio output. On the other hand, advertisements can have benefits. Local advertising on a local station can raise awareness of local events and services and can also contribute to the 'localness' of the station. By advertising goods and services designed for the target audience, adverts also help to establish station identity. And finally, reliance on commercial revenue means that the radio station is not answerable to some other source, such as the government or a church.

FURTHER READING

Starkey provides a good descriptive account of UK advertising (Starkey, 2004a: 143–65) and there are useful references to advertising throughout Hendy (2000). For an historical account see Hilmes (1997) for the American experience and Street (2006a: 76–115) on pre-war British radio advertising and sponsorship.

advertising

Commercialism

> **Commercialism refers to the development and impact of running radio stations and services as a business as opposed to a public service.**

If we categorise all radio we can see that there are public service, community, state run and commercial operations. Public service broadcasting has mainly existed in Europe but almost all US radio is commercial and has been since the 1920s. In the UK today there is a mix of public service radio (the BBC), commercial radio and a small but growing community sector. Commercial radio is of course defined by the way it is paid for and its declared goal, to make a profit. This does not mean that commercial radio is in any way inferior to the BBC, for example, but the pressures to maximise profits are noticeable sometimes. Almost all commercial radio is subject to state regulation but this has considerably decreased in the USA and the UK since the implementation of free market, less interventionist policies in those countries since the 1980s.

Commercial radio is particularly subject to the forces of commercialism, that is to say the relentless drive to cut costs and increase profits, which in the current era of capitalist media usually means the creation of huge media conglomerates and the reduction of costs through automation. The importance of this process for radio producers and students is the impact on the quality of programming and, more worryingly, commercial radio's ability to keep listeners informed of local and national political events and issues.

In the early years of radio in the USA, up to 1925, the question of how to pay for the service was a constant source of discussion. If we imagine the rather chaotic situation where stations had been set up in food stores, local newspaper offices, universities and so on and where most of the performers on radio were unreliable amateurs, it is perhaps not surprising that there was no agreed to way to make radio pay. The point was well made in 1924 by T.J. Dillion, the Managing Editor of the *Minneapolis Tribune*: 'What is the good of a newspaper running a radio? We decided that the return in good will was not worth the expense involved' (quoted in Smulyan, 1994: 40).

The solution was far from clear and as late as 1925 payment by subscription and a licence fee were both still being considered. However, despite the widespread reservations, the sponsorship of individual programmes by companies selling products became a distinctive feature of American radio. One of the earliest sponsored shows was the *Happiness Boys* on New York's WEAF who were sponsored by the Happiness Candy Company from 1923 (Smulyan, 1994: 98). Famously, the sponsorship of *Clara, Lu and Em* in 1931 by Super Suds detergent inspired the term 'soap opera' (see the entry on **Advertising**). Other well known examples are the National Carbon Company's sponsorship of *The Eveready Hour* and Cliquot Club Ginger Ale's *Cliquot Club Eskimos*. But the arguments about advertising and sponsorship on radio became part of an ideological battle between those who favoured public service broadcasting and those who wanted commercial radio. This debate ran alongside the creation of the American radio networks NBC and CBS. As these grew in importance and provided programmes for radio stations over telephone lines and as the potential to advertise to growing audiences was realised so the debate continued. The dilemma really came down to balancing the desire to exploit the huge audience of the female purchasers of most household items with the need to convince regulators that radio was a serious and worthwhile enterprise:

> The commercial broadcasters had to convince the public and public officials that they were firmly committed to high-grade cultural and educational programming ... establishing a commitment to cultural programming was seen as being of fundamental importance in keeping increased government regulation or even radical reform at bay. (Robert McChesney, in Hilmes, 1997: 13)

The enormous commercial success of pre-war commercial radio was not matched by the experience after the war. In both the USA and the UK, the arrival of television proved to be a major blow. In the American broadcasting networks, and to an extent at the BBC, investment was directed away from radio to the exciting new world of television: 'As television's picture strengthened, radio's voice began to fade' (Hilmes, 2002: 3). To make matters worse, many of the most famous radio performers moved over from radio to television. But commercial radio managed to survive in the USA because of two related developments. The invention of the transistor radio led to the manufacture of relatively cheap, portable receivers and this happily coincided with the arrival of rock and roll and the phenomenon of DJ-led youth-oriented radio (see the entry on **Reception**). The influence of commercialism is well illustrated by the development of early music radio. In the late 1950s a station manager and a programme controller sitting in a bar in Omaha noticed how the same songs were played repeatedly on the jukebox. This led them to introduce a policy of playing the 40 most popular songs (or 'singles') with the top 10 being played the most on a system of 'high rotation'. Arguably, contemporary hits radio or top 40 radio (as the format came to be known) was the result of a simple commercial decision to maximise audiences. Another device, also the result of commercial pressure, was the invention of the station 'ident' (or identification jingle):

> In heavy competition for listeners' attention, developing a consistent station image became important. Station identification jingles were heavily used by early Top 40 operators to solidify the impression that their stations were bright, lively, energetic, even irreverent places on the dial – far different from the staid, slow, proper sound of the old-line network affiliates they were competing against. (MacFarland, 1997: 67)

Although the British radio story is quite different from the American one, commercial forces still had a major influence and continue to do so today. It is often wrongly thought that only the BBC broadcast to British audiences before the Second World War. In fact there were a number of commercial radio stations broadcasting sponsored programmes from stations based on mainland Europe, including Radios Normandy and Luxembourg. The popularity of those stations with their populist mix of band music and comedy was much lighter than the rather stuffy BBC. This success encouraged the BBC to introduce the Light Programme after the war. Similarly, the extraordinary success of pop music **pirate radio** in the 1960s, when a station broadcasting from a ship moored off the English coastline transmitted pop music to Britain's youth, resulted in the BBC creating its own pop music network, BBC Radio 1, in 1967.

Probably the most important development to effect commercialism in radio was the rise of free market policies in the USA and the UK in the 1980s. Prime Minister Margaret Thatcher and President Ronald Reagan both promoted policies that were influenced by a belief in the merits of an unregulated market place. Companies should be allowed to make profits and act as they wished and it was not for the state to intervene to make things better. The impact on radio was dramatic: the Broadcasting Act of 1990 in the UK and the 1996 Telecommunications Act in the USA both radically reduced regulatory control over radio, which made commercial pressures on production even greater and had serious consequences for the quality and diversity of radio, especially in the USA.

One of the principle effects of deregulation has been to increase the number of radio stations. In towns and cities in both the USA and the

key concepts in
radio studies

UK, and in other countries where deregulation has occurred, most notably New Zealand, the rise in the number of local commercial radio stations has been exponential. At the same time the ownership of these stations has become increasingly concentrated in the hands of a very few 'media conglomerates' – this is partly because deregulation includes the removal of most limits on station ownership. Once again commercial pressure, to reduce costs and increase profits, directly impacted on radio programming. It makes sense for media companies to own large numbers of stations in order to achieve economies of scale. Management, presentation talent, technical support and programming itself can be provided centrally and spread around large numbers of stations. This is a great deal easier because of the phenomenon of programme networking and the use of automated play-out and voice tracking. What may appear to be your local radio DJ is in fact hundreds of miles away and indeed pre-recorded the apparently live show last week! In this ruthlessly commercial environment the audience becomes the product, which is then sold to the advertisers (Hendy, 2000: 31). The favoured audience for radio advertisers is those aged 25–44, because of their susceptibility to radio advertising, and a favoured format is contemporary hits (or similar). The result of this commercial situation is what Hendy calls 'swarming' to certain formats and the homogenisation of commercial radio in restricted and predictable **formats**.

The case against the rampant commercialism set free in the USA by the 1996 Act is forcefully made by Hilliard and Keith. In their book *The Quieted Voice: The Rise and Demise of Localism in American Radio* (2005) they present a stark but highly persuasive case that the huge media conglomerates, companies such as Viacom and Clear Channel, used their muscle to have ownership and content regulations relaxed and then proceeded to mount 'a frontal assault on what remained of localism in US radio broadcasting' (2005: xi). In addition:

> We also attempt to show that consolidation has, at the same time, resulted in the erosion of a key aspect of American democracy: the freedom of Americans to receive a diversity of information, opinions, and ideas, as opposed to the control of such information by a few corporate or governmental entities as is the case in most of the rest of the world. (Hilliard and Keith, 2005: xiii)

They argue that one of the reasons why radio survived the advent of television was the development of 'localism'. Programmes, including news and sport, were about the local area and often featured local people and local talent. When conglomerates take over, however, the impact is devastating. Respected local personality presenters are sacked, local programming is removed and replaced by content created hundreds or even thousands of miles away. The idea of a 'hometown radio station' has been destroyed and with it the capacity of radio to create an informed and critical electorate. Radio companies kill off any local programming for reasons of cost. Political content, and especially anything which might shed a light on the dangers of concentrated media ownership, is wiped out.

The radio landscape is not quite as bleak as this assessment suggests. The acute failures of commercial radio in the USA and the UK resulting from the essentially commercial profit maximising consequences of conglomeration and automation have created opportunities for other types of radio. In the UK the demise of commercial local radio has opened new opportunities for BBC local radio, community radio and radio over the Internet. Although the chill winds of commercialism (especially cost cutting and audience maximisation) also blow around these radio sectors, they can be partially offset by alternative sources of funding and a different philosophy of radio.

FURTHER READING

Smulyan's (1994) discussion of the 'selling of American radio' is an interesting starting point, as is Hendy (2000: 24–48). A more recent, and very outspoken, attack on the damaging commercialism of American radio is provided by Hilliard and Keith (2005), a book that contains some excellent source material.

Community Radio

Community radio places a priority on providing for the social and cultural needs of a defined community, usually in opposition to mainstream media.

There are two different ways in which the word community is used in relation to radio. 'Community radio' refers to an institutional variation normally differentiated from *commercial* and *public service radio*. Much has also been said about the 'community of listeners' who share the experience of listening to the same radio output and may feel part of *listening community*. It was the intention to combine these two uses of community in one entry and show how they are connected, but so much has been written about both community radio and listening communities that that idea had to be rejected; the entry would have quite simply been too long (see entries on **Co-presence** and **Imagined Community**).

How do we define community radio? Unfortunately, stating that it is radio specifically designed to meet the needs of the community will not do. Mainstream radio may also claim to meet those needs and may indeed be right. Similarly 'small-scale', 'alternative' and 'socially benefi-cial' do not define community radio as these can also be characteristics of commercial and public service radio. Gordon summarises the diffi-culties of definition:

> Just a little research in the area of community radio shows that anybody with any kind of interest in radio knows exactly what community radio is. Ironically, almost everybody disagrees. Very strong views are held about community radio. There seems to be a general consensus that a community station is a radio station, run primarily by volunteers on a not-for-profit basis, but that seems to be where the agreement ends. (Gordon, 2006: 26)

It follows that attempting a really convincing definition of what has become one of the most interesting and rewarding areas of study within radio is beset with problems. It seems, however, to be generally agreed that community radio stations place a priority on their relationship with an identified community and attempt to satisfy the perceived social and cultural needs of that group. This two defining characteristic of community radio can be seen if we look at some of the examples of the sector dis-cussed in a growing body of research.

One of the most extraordinary and celebrated examples of community radio is the case of the tiny stations set up by miners in Bolivia from 1947 onwards. Not unlike their counterparts in other parts of the world, the Bolivian miners were self-disciplined and self-educated with a particular interest in technology. In the three to four decades of their existence Bolivia was ruled by military dictatorships under which the media was severely restricted. The miners' radio stations satisfied a desire for gen-uinely alternative media with 'an absolutely heroic record in refusing to be silenced by even the most right-wing and ruthless military coups' (O'Connor, 2004: 1). In 1971 the dictator Hugo Banzer closed the stations but they were resurrected and formed a vital part of the democratic resistance to the coup of 1980. The miners' radio stations were unusual in being entirely created and funded not by a charity or outside agency but by the miners and their families. They were created by an oppressed community and helped promote not only democracy but also the local language (Quecha) and the oral tradition. As an example of community radio, the Bolivian radio stations are pretty well definitive. Radical, local and meeting specific cultural and political needs: truly this was radio embedded in the local community created by and for local people.

At about the same times as the first Bolivian miners' radio station started broadcasting, the American radio visionary Lewis Hill founded KPFA in Berkley, California. This community radio station was part of a network of five stations in different parts of the USA created by the Pacifica Foundation, which aimed in its founding statement to:

> ... engage in any activity that shall contribute to a lasting understanding between nations and between the individuals of all nations, races, creeds and colors; to gather and disseminate information on the causes of conflict between any and all such groups. (Land, 1999: 41)

As an example of radical community radio the Pacifica case was certainly alternative, inspired by the pacifism of its founder and against the militarism of the Cold War era. The Pacifica stations went on to play a vital role in the anti-Vietnam war movement as well as being pioneers of 1960s cultural and political radicalism. Whether they were genuinely 'community' radio stations depends on how we define community. They were funded by subscription and those subscribers could be seen as at least a collective of like-minded people but the New York Pacifica station WBAI was in the 1970s dominated by white, middle-class, straight men and broadcasting to a 'minuscule audience in the city's vast non-white communities' (Land, 1999: 127). If we accept Pacifica as community radio (as most commentators do) this does mean stretching the concept of community radio quite a long way.

Some of the most notable examples of community radio exist for indigenous people with their own language, sometimes illiterate and possessing a strong oral tradition, for whom radio is not only an expression of community but also a means of education and development. Radio has a particular advantage as a tool for social change and participatory communication, it is cost-efficient, an aural medium, relevant to local culture, sustainable, has good geographical reach and has the potential to converge with the Internet. It is unsurprising, therefore, that much of the literature on community radio includes the words 'radio' and 'development' in the title. Myers (2000), for example, discusses the case of Daande Duwansa (the Voice of Douentza) in Mali. A solar-powered FM radio station serving 120,000 largely illiterate listeners in the local language and supported by the UK-based charity Oxfam. This is just one example of what Myers calls an explosion in community radio in West Africa since the early 1990s. Daande Duwansa features health, education, agriculture and 'women's issues' and succeeds partly because there is no television in the area and no competition from the press. Other examples of indigenous community radio include stations providing for Australian Aboriginal people and similar stations for the Inuit people of Northern Canada. Writing about the latter example, Alia comments 'in a country dotted with remote communities, radio is the friendliest, most useful and most available medium' (2004: 78). Here, community radio plays an important role in one-to-one communication connecting people who share Inuit language and culture.

In a fascinating and important discussion of local commercial radio in Turkey, Algan describes the way young Turkish men and women use radio to date each other and send personal messages (Algan, 2005). In the town of Sanliurfa marriages are arranged and there is little room for romance. Young people can be severely punished for breaking with tradition and in the most extreme cases there are 'honour killings' for those who disobey. Local radio offers a way of sending secret messages outside the gaze of family elders. A 'youth community of the air' exists in which love and criticism of social norms makes commercial radio a genuinely radical alternative to mainstream culture. There are three interesting aspects of this case study: first, in a sense it defies the orthodox view of community radio by being a commercial radio station (Radyo Tempo); second, it is not about development; and, third, it directly challenges rather than affirms the local culture and community norms. Radyo Tempo serves as an important reminder of the *diversity* of community radio and the danger of using simplistic definitions to describe it.

Community radio is a richly diverse part of global media as these very few examples have shown. In Britain the regulatory bodies the Radio Authority and its replacement Ofcom have introduced a 'third tier' of radio by rolling out community radio across the UK. At the time of writing there are 104 UK community stations on air with another 70 pending. This has become a dynamic part of the UK radio landscape with important implications for radio studies. There is a strong whiff of public service, however, in this new initiative in which 'social gain' is given far greater prominence than 'radio' in the official literature. A far cry from the Bolivian miners' radio station ringed by dynamite in a doomed and desperate attempt to keep the army out or late night explicit sex talk on bilingual Radio Zimbabwe (Mano, 2005). But community radio is a very broad category. It can be found on both commercial and public service radio (in Britain, especially on BBC local radio) as well as on subscription or donor-funded stations. It can serve tiny geographically isolated or close-knit communities, which conform to stereotypical or even nostalgic ideas of community or to dispersed communities or 'diasporas'.

FURTHER READING

This is a dynamic area of research and debate with some excellent up-to-date material available online. O'Connor's (2004) account of Bolivian miners' stations is something of a classic and more recently, Algan's (2005) article on Turkish commercial community radio is fascinating. Gordon's (2006) comparison of UK and Australian stations is detailed and informative.

Convergence

> *The word 'convergence' is used in a variety of ways but principally to describe the interchangeability of different media platforms; so, for example, radio and the Internet might deliver the same, similar or complimentary content.*

The term 'convergence' has become one of the most important and widely used terms in media studies. It is used to describe a variety of different processes in contemporary digital media, including the convergence of media companies into conglomerates, the interchangeability of different media platforms and the delivery of the same content on different media.

Convergence in the media industry itself, whereby individual media giants own a variety of different media outlets, is of course a defining feature of the industry. Many of the global media conglomerates are mainly based in the USA, including Viacom, AOL-Time Warner, Clear Channel Communications and News Corporation. The increased concentration of ownership is a characteristic of advanced capitalism and closely associated with the emergence of globalisation which itself is greatly facilitated by the Internet. It is now much easier for a conglomerate to have production facilities and outlets around the world and to take advantage of cheap labour or low tax economies. This industry convergence has been facilitated by relaxation of rules on media ownership (for example in the USA the Telecommunications Act 1996). Together, these factors have produced a highly concentrated radio industry in which some companies own hundreds (and in the case of Clear Channel over a thousand) radio stations. This process of convergence has not been without opposition as these words, spoken in a debate in the US Congress, testify:

> And it will be very dangerous for this country when a tiny number of multi-multibillion-dollar international conglomerates own virtually all of our newspapers, all of our radio stations, all of our television stations, all of our book publishing companies, all of the companies that produce the films that we observe. (Congressman Bernie Sanders, quoted in Hilliard and Keith, 2005: 107)

The reason why industry convergence is perceived as a threat is because of its impact on the diversity of views expressed in the media and the marginalisation of minority groups. The mighty Clear Channel actively supported President Bush's policy on Iraq by organising pro-invasion rallies in 2003, raising questions about political influence on output in its 1214 radio stations (Albarran, 2004: 341). While the Dixie Chicks were banned from Cumulus and other radio stations because one of the band criticised Bush over Iraq, the right-wing, pro-war presenters of talk radio increasingly dominated the airwaves. Furthermore the impact of this concentration of media ownership has reduced the local quality of US radio and marginalised non-white groups (Hilliard and Keith, 2005).

It is, perhaps, in the area of platform convergence that radio has been most affected. This form of convergence refers to 'the blurring of the distinction between telecommunications, computers, radio, television and newspapers [which] has been made possible by digital technology' (Franklin et al., 2005: 49). In the specific case of radio there is some convergence with television but it is the relationship between radio and the Internet that is the more important. So a radio station might be 'simulcast' as a live stream over the Internet to reach a global audience or it might use the Internet to provide an audio on demand service, for example of previously broadcast output. There might be background information about a station on the Internet, such as pictures of DJs, interviews with performers or places for listener chat. Putting a webcam in a radio studio is increasingly common and this creates a convergence not only with the Internet but also with television, as the radio show may look like a television programme. MP3 technology has greatly added to convergence. A podcast of a radio programme can be made available as a download for an MP3 player. Alternatively, a newspaper journalist might use the production techniques and skills of radio to produce a podcast that is at least radio-like. Platform convergence is further enhanced when audio and video are accessible on a mobile phone; here the distinctions between the conventional categories of radio, film and television start to break down completely.

Anther aspect of convergence is its impact on production. In the case of fiction the same work might be produced for publication as a book but also as a radio play or audio book and as a film (for example *Lord of the Rings* and the Harry Potter books). In the case of news and current affairs on the BBC, convergence takes the form of 'bi-media' production. The same interview or report from a correspondent might appear on television and radio. This 'journalism factory' approach to news gathering can produce cost savings but at the expense sometimes of the quality of radio journalism which is so much more reliant on the spoken word.

key concepts in radio studies

FURTHER READING

Although this is likely to be the subject of more writing in the future, the literature available now on radio-specific convergence is quite limited. Hendy (2000: 46–59) provides a useful introduction and Berry's (2006) interesting article discusses the convergent phenomenon of podcasting. Hilliard and Keith (2005) is a thought-provoking discussion of industry convergence.

Formats

The radio format refers to the programming policy of a radio station, normally defined by the type of music played.

Radio formats are a means of producing a standardised and predictable output for listeners and are mainly, but not exclusively, associated with commercial radio. Formatting is designed to satisfy the needs of advertisers, 'a standardised product is likely to be the best means of predictably securing a given audience – an audience which is drawn to a certain station or programme by the promise of a given product' (Hendy, 2000: 95). Radio formats include standardisation of programmes, the daily programme schedule and the station format itself. This entry will concentrate on the last of these.

The radio format emerged in the USA in the 1950s when competition from television posed a particular threat. Before the 1950s, radio stations had offered mixed programming which included music, drama, news, comedy, sport and so on. These often locally based radio stations, however, faced stiff competition from television and newly established stations. One solution was to feature hit records from the record charts, and the top 40 format quickly became dominant in the USA. As competition for audiences intensified stations refined the music format by using playlists, which placed different emphases on contemporary and older music. The closest format to mainstream top 40 was contemporary hits radio (CHR) and this was joined by a truly bewildering array of subtly different varieties: adult contemporary (AC), adult oriented rock (AOR) and more recently hot AC, mainstream AC, soft AC and so on. Other successful formats include country, oldie, middle of the road, jazz, gospel, news, talk and various ethnically based stations.

Radio formats reflect an approach to radio programming that is based on the belief that radio is a business like any other and the only criteria by which to judge a radio station is the number of listeners who are 'sold' to the advertisers. The language surrounding the radio format is the discourse of marketing and branding and audience demographics. It is also based on the principle that the radio audience can be segmented into niches, these targets are then given the programming which research suggests they want. This approach fits well with the commercial radio environment in the USA and especially since the deregulation of ownership in the 1990s. Because one company might own most of the radio stations in a single town or city, the use of formats helps differentiate their output. The US radio industry regularly congratulates itself on ghettoising the audience in this way and supplying such diversity of station formats. The reality, as Douglas has pointed out, may be very different:

> There are currently something of the order of fifty officially listed formats, and the hairsplitting between them seems ridiculous to an outsider. What really is the difference between soft rock ('plays older, softer rock') and soft adult contemporary ('recurrents mixed with some current music')? Classic hits features ''70s and '80s hits from rock-based artists,' while classic rock features 'older rock cuts'. (1999: 348)

Douglas goes on chastise the industry for using formats to keep any kind of variety 'outside the door'. Americans, she argues, want safe 'gated-in listening' in the same way that they want to live in gated communities. Perhaps this search for safety in music explains why the country format has become one of the most popular music formats in the USA. More than any other musical genre, country music reflects mainstream American values and is often safely tuneful and easy listening. The rise of country reflected changing cultural values in the 1980s and 1990s and especially the morally conservative and Christian values espoused at the time:

> Country provided a 'safe' image when compared to pop music's excursions to the ghetto for rap or the leather bands for grunge rock. Americans faced no fear when confronted with kids in cowboy hats. (Ed Shane, in MacFarland, 1997: 75)

While the formatting of radio, and especially radio stations, has been a particular characteristic of radio in America it has also influenced British radio and even the BBC. In the 1960s the different radio 'networks' of the BBC offered quite mixed programming, so news, drama and music for example could be heard on the Home Service but also the Third and the Light Programmes. In 1967, the pop music network, BBC Radio 1, was launched and with its highly specialised programming was the most formatted of the four networks. Two years later the policy document *Broadcasting in the Seventies* spelt out the reasons for an increased formatting of the networks:

It recognized ... that in the face of television radio had 'lost is compulsiveness', and that few listeners any longer bother to look at the printed schedules in their daily papers or in the *Radio Times*. In the face of this strictly casual approach to radio, it argued that each of the four networks needed to offer services 'with a definite and recognisable programme character', so that listeners could tune in with a 'reasonable expectation of getting *what* they wanted, and knowing *when* they could expect it. (Hendy, 2007: 53, original emphasis)

The quote above articulates well the pressure to create greater conformity and predictability in radio output, felt even in the non-commercial and public service BBC. There clearly is an audience expectation to hear something predictable when they tune to a particular station. The danger of this, as Douglas points out, is the loss of originality and the unexpected in what we hear.

FURTHER READING

Hendy (2000: 94–110) provides a useful introduction to the concept. A more recent discussion of the application of radio formats in the UK is in Starkey (2004a: 89–109). For a passionate critique of formatted radio see Douglas (1999).

Internet Radio

> **Internet radio is radio made accessible over the Internet, either as live streamed audio or as audio on demand.**

There are some quite obvious facts about Internet (or 'web') radio, which are worth stating at the beginning. Because it is communicated over the Internet it is globally available, largely unregulated and unrestricted in quantity (unlike analogue and digital radio which compete for parts of the spectrum or of a multiplex). To put it slightly differently, a web radio station can be set up by an amateur enthusiast in their proverbial bedroom for very little cost without worrying about the regulatory machinery of the state. Have we, in other words, returned to the world of the pre-broadcasting era when the amateur ruled? The discussion that follows suggests that it is not quite as easy as that.

The Internet is primarily a visual medium. As Chris Priestman points out, the Internet is largely text based and visual and indeed 'demands even more visual concentration than watching television' whereas radio is non-visual (2002: 44). If this is the case how does radio make use of the World Wide Web? The answer to this question must inevitably draw on existing and previous examples of web radio and these suggest that what might be called terrestrial radio has not fundamentally changed or been transformed by the Internet but that it has exploited the opportunities for greater interactivity and for reaching new audiences that the Internet provides.

Internet radio was made possible by the invention of Internet streaming technology in the early 1990s. This meant that users could listen to radio in real time without having to download an audio file first. The breakthrough in this technology was achieved by the American company Progressive Networks who developed the RealPlayer audio software. In 1994, the campus radio station at the University of Kansas began broadcasting over the Internet and in the following year, Internet radio was beginning to make inroads into commercial radio in the USA and beyond (van Selm et al., 2004: 266). The growth of web radio can partly be attributed to its appeal to both established public service and commercial radio broadcasters as well as its appeal to alternative or unlicensed enthusiasts or 'hobbyists' who suddenly found an opportunity to make radio without the need for either a lot of money or the approval of regulators.

Established radio stations have tended to use the Internet to simultaneously broadcast (or 'simulcast') their normal output. Programming originally available to a restricted local or national audience suddenly achieves a global reach. In addition, a relatively young audience who use computers a lot of the time, possibly at work or as students, can listen to web radio while 'multitasking'. Research in the USA of early adopters of web radio found that these listeners (referred to as 'streamies') were a particularly attractive group of well educated young Internet users who were happy to click on web ads to make online purchases (Anderson, 2004: 756).

The way commercial radio has exploited this new opportunity does to an extent deny its earlier promise: 'The new technologies of the

Internet, at first, seem to offer a space in which music radio can be made free of corporate interests, where innovation can take place, and therefore where variety can flourish for the public good' (T. Wall, 2004: 9). However, the reality so far has been that the economic and corporate pressures that have shaped commercial (and largely music) radio have also been at work in the development of web radio. By offering a web enhancement of the standard on air service, radio stations have found new markets for advertisers. A typical model is to have a branded web site which offers simulcast output as well as archived programmes on demand and extra live celebrity interviews, ticket offers, live concerts and interactive opportunities (discussion boards and chat rooms) with web advertisements which lead to online purchases. Research by Lind and Medoff in 2000 showed that nearly three quarters of radio station web sites were mainly promotional and featured staff profiles and programming information (van Selm et al., 2004: 267).

Web radio can also appeal to public service broadcasters, especially because of its global reach and ability to provide additional information to the audio service. The best example of this is undoubtedly BBC Online, which both simulcasts the various BBC radio stations and also provides a 'listen again' archive facility. The BBC's web radio is provided in conjunction with the huge BBC news and information web site and the overall effect reinforces the public service credentials of the organisation.

Radio Netherlands is the Dutch external service based at the public service broadcasting centre at Hilversum. This press release well illustrates the perceived benefits of web radio to a public service broadcaster:

> As an external service, Radio Netherlands sees its role as representing a reliable, balanced source of international news and European cultural information and entertainment to the rest of the world through as many platforms as possible. ... they are particularly aware of providing a point of contact for listeners from the former Dutch colonies in Indonesia and their scattered diaspora. Conversely, the station also attracts a significant North American audience among European expatriates and others. The online presence is therefore a natural extension of Radio Netherlands long experience of outward looking, international broadcasting. (Quoted in Priestman, 2002: 108)

Both the BBC and Radio Netherlands are clearly interested in using web radio to communicate their national culture and political perspective to a global audience. At the same time, the British and Dutch communities spread around the world (the 'diaspora') can listen to familiar radio and new from back home. In a study of the state radio station 'Voice of Vietnam' [VOI] Dang notes that VOV web radio is listened to by both the global Vietnamese community as well as a younger, educated audience in Vietnam (Dang, 2008). Dang shows how VOV uses the Internet to disseminate positive messages about Vietnam to the relatively wealthy ex-pat community of Vietnamese living in the West while also tempting young professionals back into the radio listening habit.

Another relevant example is that of Radio B92 in Belgrade during the Balkans War. This is an heroic example of web radio's resilience in the face of a dictatorship. Radio B92 was a licensed terrestrial radio station, which was critical of the totalitarian regime of President Milosevic. When it was eventually closed down in 1996 it began broadcasting using the new RealAudio software and so web radio played a vital part in the eventual overthrow of the Milosevic dictatorship (Priestman, 2002: 195).

A different form of web radio are those stations which are Internet only:

> These are the freestyle climbers of web radio who have no ropes to support them. They are exploring a different face of web radio than are the established broadcasters. They are finding out about the spaces that lie in between the vertices of the existing broadcasting world, where restrictions on the access to the electromagnetic spectrum and licences to transmit no longer limit the number of stations that can be on air at one time. (Priestman, 2002: 116)

In the main Internet-only stations tend to target niche audiences of like-minded listeners who share the same interest. Because of their size and the enthusiasm of their producers, these specialist stations may be providing genuinely innovative content and are also more authentically interactive than commercially based web radio.

It is difficult to make any authoritative claims for Internet radio for the simple reason that Internet and wireless technology, and the way these are used, is changing so rapidly. The portability of wireless Internet radio sets is increasing as wireless networks expand. The first prototype of an Internet radio set installed in a car was made in 2000 and since then the concept of the wireless networked workplace, campus, town or city is a reality, making web radio suddenly a great deal more portable. For Wall and others it is the interactive potential of web radio which suggests it will continue in some or other. The future may be 'bespoke' programming reflecting the exact music tastes of the individual listener, paid for by subscription. This could be done using high-quality MP3 music files. This suggests a fusion of different uses of the Internet including the social spaces (such as 'My Space') where sound and images can be combined for others to see. Internet social spaces need not replace web radio, which surely will survive in its role to compliment established commercial and public service radio stations. It is in the sphere of personal and bespoke web radio that the greatest potential and uncertainty lies.

FURTHER READING

Anything published on Internet radio is likely to at least appear out-of-date by the time it is published. However, there are some useful early statements about Internet radio that the reader has to update by adding more recent examples. Priestman (2002) is an excellent introduction and remains surprisingly relevant. The short article on Dutch Internet radio by van Selm et al. (2004) provides an interesting case study. T. Wall (2004) on the Internet and music is also useful.

Localism

> *Localism refers to the specifically local quality of some radio stations, often expressed by their coverage of local events.*

Historically radio began as a local phenomenon. KDKA in Pittsburgh in 1920, arguably the first radio station, was very much a local service with a 100-watt transmitter and a range of less than 40 miles. Even the mighty BBC began life in 1922 as a group of local stations and only became more regional from 1928. The growth of the radio networks in the USA and a centralised BBC in Britain made radio increasingly national and less local. More recently, the growth of media conglomerates on both sides of the Atlantic has tended to further diminish local radio although in recent years there have signs of its rebirth in the form of community and micro broadcasting.

The term 'localism' is increasingly used to describe positive, but often declining, features of local radio. There is no clearly articulated definition of localism (or 'localness') to which we can turn although the regulators, for example the Office of Communications (Ofcom) in the UK, have operational guidelines that at least contribute to our understanding. At a general or abstract level, radio localism refers to the degree to which a station's output is locally sourced and reflects the needs, interests and culture of the local community. Being more specific, local sourcing might include a station's studio being sited in the community and locally made programmes featuring local people. In terms of content, localism might be seen in local news stories. In addition, local weather and travel news, local events and information about pending disasters, coverage of local cultural and sporting events would also contribute to localism. Other slightly less tangible features might be the participation of local people in programmes and with this the sound of local accents and dialects. In multicultural areas, a 'localist' station would reflect the diversity of communities, cultures and voices.

The recent British experience of local radio dates back to 1967, in the case of BBC local radio, and 1973 with the introduction of commercial local radio. Although the BBC introduced local radio to achieve the localism described here it has only been partially successful. There are 40 local radio stations but the audience has evolved into a largely 55-plus working- and lower middle-class group who are the most reliant on local services (Linfoot, 2007: 129). In addition to the problem of this narrowing of the audience the BBC's own rather patrician reputation can prevent it from engaging with local communities as Linfoot discovered in his research into three local radio community projects:

> The relationship between the communities and the BBC was sometimes uneasy. The BBC, according to the community groups, was perceived as dominant, sometimes threatening and remote (both geographically and personally) and was therefore viewed with suspicion. (Linfoot, 2007: 133)

Commercial radio in the USA provides the most important and dramatic example of localism, captured in the title of a recent book on the subject, (Hilliard and Keith, 2005). The 'rise' in the title occurred in the 1950s when the broadcasting networks effectively abandoned radio for the glittering opportunities of television. By the late 1950s, network radio was almost entirely dead but that did not mean the end of radio itself. This description of American local radio in the 1950s serves as an excellent description of localism in practice:

> As network radio declined in the early 1950s, local stations became more and more involved in programming that originated locally. These shows included local music groups, panel and quiz shows with local people, talks and public affairs programs with local personalities, and documentaries, docudramas, and dramas relating to local history and issues and featuring local performers. Not only were radio stations addressing more and more programming to the specific needs of the community, but by producing more and more programs locally, they were involving more and more local people in the station's operations. (Hilliard and Keith, 2005: 56)

The halcyon days of local radio were not to last as the gradual lessening of radio regulation meant that large media conglomerates could buy up local stations and centralise programming. On both sides of the Atlantic, the free market policies of the Reagan and Thatcher administrations initiated the freeing up of media ownership rules, sometimes to the benefit, it must be said, of the media barons who supported right-wing policies. The Broadcasting Act 1990 (UK) and the Telecommunications Act 1996 (USA) both had devastating effects on localism as content and ownership regulations were lifted to allow stations to remain local in name only. Following the 1996 act, 4000 of the 11,000 American radio stations were sold and bought by media giants such as Viacom and Clear Channel Communications. Aided by developments in the automation of output, formerly local and localist stations were stripped of local content and local presenters as programmes and music were piped out of remote production centres. Local news often largely disappeared along with local sports reports, local weather and of course local voices (Hilliard and Keith, 200: 79).

In Britain the decline of local content has been not quite as dramatic as in the USA partly because of continued regulation. The Ofcom (2004) document on preparing for the future of radio recommends that every local station has a full-time journalist, responds to local events in a 'timely' manner and also has a studio located in the area. British commercial radio, however, is subject to the same business approaches as radio elsewhere and the use of networking and automation (including voice tracking and automated playlists) have made local references in commercial radio sound more like symbolic responses to regulation than any genuine attempt to respond to the local community.

localism

The question of radio localism is a complex one. On the one hand, there are the commercial imperatives of the global media conglomerates obliterating what little is left of localism. On the other, is the recent growth of community and micro radio, which both respond to the centralisation and uniformity of commercial radio, Internet radio and the phenomenon of podcasting are also locally sourced or amateur alternatives to the professional mainstream. For those who believe that localism is a democratic bulwark against the propagandist, Republican-supporting, centralised commercial radio (Hilliard and Keith, 2005: 79) the micro/community radio movement, together with various Internet-based alternatives, do give reasons for hope.

It would be wrong to leave this subject without briefly reflecting on an issue for both local and community radio, the evolving nature of community itself. The small town in 1950s America was the home of what was perhaps the most genuinely localist radio. In the world of the 21st century, however, people are far more geographically mobile and exposed to far greater national and global media. To take just one example, the global branding of sport may make coverage of the geographically local sports team irrelevant to the majority of a local population who are far more interested in what happens to Manchester United. The very idea of a stable, geographically determined community with shared values and interests is problematic as communities of interest, and the media which serve them, become more important.

FURTHER READING

The American story of radio localism is discussed in a politically charged but nonetheless extremely interesting book by Hilliard and Keith (2005), revealingly subtitled *The Rise and Demise of Localism in American Radio*. The report on the future of British radio by the telecommunications regulator is very revealing (Ofcom, 2004). BBC local radio is examined in some detail by Linfoot (2007).

Micro Radio

Micro radio is an American development in which low-power radio transmitters are used often to transmit an alternative message to mainstream media.

Unlicensed radio has taken different forms in the USA and the UK. In Britain, the offshore radio pirates of the 1960s have been the most important expression of unregulated broadcasting while in America, low-power FM stations, also called 'micro radio', have been the most important symbol of audio defiance.

The history of micro radio in the USA is a particularly complicated story of regulation and defiance with the established broadcasters (the National Association of Broadcasters and National Public Radio) on the one hand and the micro broadcasters on the other, described by one commentator as 'an exceedingly diverse lot' (Riismandel, 2002: 426). In between these two camps is the regulator, the FCC, opting at different times for a pro or anti position.

So what exactly is micro radio and why does it exist? In the USA most commercial radio stations operate on FM and have transmitters of between 1000 and 100,000 watts in power. The greater the power of the transmitter the farther away the radio station can be heard. There are, however, small, even portable transmitters that can be bought for a few hundred dollars and use less than 100 watts of power right down to one watt. These transmitters may only reach audiences in a relatively very small radius but they are often used in an urban setting with blocks of accommodation that might include thousands of potential listeners.

From the 1980s onwards, the potential of low-power FM was seized upon by a very loose and diverse coalition which is often referred to as the 'micro radio movement'.

> The modern micro broadcasting movement began on November 25, 1986 in a public housing development in Springfield, IL. Put on the air for about $600, the one watt station broadcast openly on 107.1 FM as Black Liberation Radio (now Human rights Radio). The operator, Mbanna Kantako, a legally blind African-American in his mid-thirties, started the station because he felt that the African-American community in Springfield was not being served by the local media. (Adams and Phipps, 2004: 885)

This was just the start of a rapid expansion in unlicensed micro radio, the product of a variety of factors at the time. Perhaps the most important of these was the consolidation and centralisation of commercial radio. The huge media conglomerates, including Clear Channel and Viacom, had made radio a centralised operation, 'the end result for listeners and communities is that radio stations fail to reflect their local communities very well, giving especially short shrift to local news and issues ...' (Riismandel, 2004: 424). Along with the removal of local content was a form of censorship that denied access to the airwaves for part of the population, the 'squelching of unpopular and dissident voices' as Riismandel puts it.

Another factor that made growth of micro radio possible was the increased availability of cheap, lightweight transmitters. The alternative of getting a radio licence was impossibly expensive for most potential broadcasters and this made the unlicensed route yet more appealing. Added to this was the example of Free Radio Berkeley and the pioneer of micro radio, Stephen Paul Dunifer. FRB first broadcast in April 1992 at a hippy gathering. The schedule included anti-war messages, left-wing politics and music. At times the equipment was carried in backpacks and FRB was transmitted from the Berkely Hills to avoid the police. Dunifer became a crusader for micro radio and sold low-power transmitters compete with instructions over the Internet.

Some of the groups attracted to micro radio in the 1990s were often those who were quite simply excluded from the media. The Spanish-speaking community for example has its own language, musical tastes and political priorities. Radio Marantha in Cleveland, Free Radio Santa Cruz and Radio Zapata all provided for Hispanic needs. Radio Zapata, in Salinas, California, was run mainly by Spanish-speaking strawberry pickers: it played music from southern Mexico and actively supported a local rent strike (Walker, 2001: 223). In Florida in the 1990s there was a particularly active micro radio scene with stations run by Christian evangelists, bikers, right-wingers, Greeks, reggae and hip hop fans.

Throughout its short history, micro radio has been vociferously opposed by the establishment; commercial radio and NPR. They have both encouraged the FCC to stop micro radio and certainly not to license it. Their argument, unsurprisingly, has been that unlicensed radio creates interference for licensed stations as well as defending the service they provide. Despite their lobbying, the FCC introduced a licensed low-power service in 2000 for stations to transmit using 10-, 100- and 1000-watt transmitters. The FCC's move is very similar to the launch of community radio in Britain in 2002 by Ofcom, the UK regulator, and both developments seem to reflect concern about the decline of local-ism and diversity in mainstream radio. Both micro radio and community radio have the potential to bring a diversity of voices to the microphone. As Riismandel has expressed it, 'the lack of variability in voice, accent, and dialect is really just a symptom of the overwhelming homogeneity and lack of diversity in American radio broadcasting' (2002: 427). Micro radio, licensed or not, clearly has the potential to make radio more than just a place where we can hear professional broadcasters or the edited and controlled voices of callers to radio stations.

The encyclopaedia entry by Adams and Phipps (2004) is a very clear starting point for further reading. Riismandel (2002) explores the controversial nature of low-power FM and its rebirth. Walker's (2001) book is a colourful description of the radio rebels on micro radio.

Pirate Radio

> *Pirate radio is unlicensed radio and the term is mainly associated with the historically specific case of offshore radio in Britain in the 1960s.*

The term 'pirate radio' suggests the romance of determined, but illegal, radio enthusiasts transmitting exciting alternatives to dull mainstream stations. To add to this romance, the famous British offshore pirates of the 1960s actually transmitted from ships tossed on the waves of the North Sea to the bedrooms of their largely teenage listeners.

Street defines pirate radio as follows: 'The term is used to denote a form of sound broadcasting contravening licensing regulations either within the county of origin, or reception or both' (2006b: 206). There are plenty of examples of this form of piracy in both the UK and the USA but I am going to suggest here that it is useful to think of radio piracy as a specifically British phenomenon, mainly associated with the 1960s offshore stations and more recently with illegal stations based in the inner city. In doing this I am excluding 'border radio' and '**micro**' **radio**; the last two are discussed in separate entries. Border radio refers to Mexico-based stations, often with extremely powerful transmitters, broadcasting into the USA (and sometimes as far as Chicago) from the 1930s to the 1980s. These stations broadcast a strange combination of advertisements for quack medicines, hell-raising preachers and some of the first broadcasts of country and rock music to be heard in the USA. The legendary DJ Wolfman Jack first appeared on the border station XERF in 1963 on a show which featured rock and blues and the Wolfman's 'superjock' persona. Border radio has been called 'outlaw' radio but the term 'pirate' seems to be particularly British and so although there are clear similarities between border radio and the 1960s British pirates it is best to use the term only for the latter.

In Britain in the 1930s the BBC was a monopoly and there were no rivals apart from those stations based in Europe providing an English language commercial service. Of these only Radio Luxembourg was technically a pirate station because it was illegally using the wavelength allocated to Warsaw Radio, whereas the others, such as Radio Normandy and Radio Toulouse, were not breaking the law either in Europe or in Britain (Street, 2006a: 206). There were a number of illegal broadcasters, however, based in Britain, mainly amateurs carrying on the tradition of amateur broadcasting which had started before the First World War. Gerald Barker transmitted illegally from Norwich as the 'Old Pirate' and was closed down in 1934; this is probably the origin of the term (Skues, 1994: 14).

After the Second World War the BBC's monopoly continued but by this time there were three radio networks (the Home Service, the Light Programme and the Third Programme) which provided greater choice for listeners. A number of factors conspired to make the offshore pirates an extremely successful and important stage in the development of British radio. In the 1950s and early 1960s the mood in Britain was changing: old deferential values were losing their grip and a more tolerant and liberal climate prevailed. The *Goon Show* poked fun at the establishment and tradition: on television *That Was the Week That Was* was controversially satirical and mocked members of the Conservative Government. The BBC was largely incapable of playing the new rock and pop music that Britain's youth wanted to hear, limitations on 'needle time' (the amount of air time for playing records) were the result of arrangements between the BBC and the Musicians' Union and, in addition, the decidedly traditional managers of the BBC were not impressed by the new music. A final ingredient that made pirate radio possible was the fact that British legal jurisdiction ended three miles out to sea. What followed, described here by Street, is radio history:

> On Sunday, 29 March 1964 Radio Caroline, the brainchild of a young Irish entrepreneur, Ronan O'Rahilly, made its first broadcast from international waters five miles off Harwich. There followed an explosion in such stations which radically changed the course of youth-music radio culture in Britain, and ultimately prompted the BBC to create Radio One in 1967. This was American-style, DJ-fronted popular music radio of a style largely unheard of in Britain, and directly confrontational to the BBC's post-war policy. (Street, 2006a: 202)

Radio Caroline opened with the Rolling Stones hit *Not Fade Away*. In the following month Radio Atlanta became the second pirate radio station and they were joined in December 1964 by Radio London. At their peak there were 21 pirates, playing the music of the 1960s to an audience hungry for new music and the American-influenced, cool style of DJ presentation. The pre-eminent British radio DJ John Peel, after a spell working in the USA, was a Radio London DJ (in his partly finished autobiography, Peel described driving through the Texas night listening to Wolfman Jack from over the border in Mexico). His late night show *The Perfumed Garden* brought American rock, including the Grateful Dead, Jefferson Airship and Frank Zappa to British audiences. There can be no doubt that pirate radio was an important opportunity for British DJs to develop their presentational style. Peel was famous for ignoring the play-list in favour of his own eclectic but visionary choice of music. He also helped the off-air recorders at home by not talking over the music. Another pirate legend was Kenny Everett, also on Radio London, who pioneered the creative and innovative use of pre-recording in his shows.

Pirate radio was abruptly brought to an end by the oddly titled *Marine etc., Broadcasting (Offences) Bill*, which was implemented on 14 August 1967 and in effect prohibited them. At the same time, the BBC established its new network for pop music, BBC Radio 1, which systematically employed many of the star DJs from the pirate radio stations, including Peel and Everett.

BBC Radio 1 and the growth of local radio in the UK soon afterwards, both BBC and commercial, quickly filled the space left by the demise of the pirates. There has, however, been a small revival in radio piracy in the form of illegal radio stations, often playing hip-hop and urban music and based in the ethnic minority communities of cities in the UK. Some of these pirate stations have been made legitimate by the growth of community radio since 2005. A good example of a station that was pirate but then became legitimate is Kiss FM, which was an illegal station in the mid-1980s and then won a licence and is now one of London's most successful music stations.

Pirate radio is important as an example of how liberation from regulatory control, and the restrictive practices of the BBC, made a new and innovative style of music radio, and a whole raft of new music, a possibility. Historically it has often been the case that illegal broadcasting has been the catalyst for change. So border radio pioneered country, blues and rock music in the USA and British pirates were clearly essential for the development of youth-oriented pop music radio in the 1960s. It is worth briefly mentioning piracy in Africa, to take just one example from the rest of the world. In Mali, West Africa, in the 1990s there were dozens, if not hundreds, of illegal radio stations broadcasting to a largely non-literate audience at a time of democratisation. In some cases, although the pirates were closed down, they inspired the creation of legitimate community radio stations. Once again, pirate radio had pointed the way for legitimate radio.

FURTHER READING

One of the most detailed accounts of the development of pirate radio in the UK in the 1960s is Skues (1994). Street (2006a: 195–215) places the short career of pirate radio in the wider context of commercial and public service radio at the time. M. Wall (2004) is just one of several books on John Peel which includes his career on pirate radio.

Regulation

> *Regulation is the process where a government organisation controls aspects of radio broadcasting including allocation of the radio spectrum, programme content and station ownership.*

The terms 'regulation' and more recently 'deregulation' are associated mainly with commercial radio and in particular with the long regulatory history of both UK and US radio. It would be reasonable to ask why it has been necessary to regulate radio at all. In Britain for example, the press barely seems to be controlled at all by government interference and regulation so why is commercial radio? Similarly we can read and see pretty much whatever we want on the Internet, a totally unregulated medium except in one or two authoritarian states, while the philosophy, funding, content, ownership, diversity, location and format of radio has all been the subject of meticulous control at some time.

As is often the case in the attempt to unravel the nature of radio, part of the answer can be found by looking at the earliest incarnation of wireless broadcasting. In the USA and the UK the fact of radio regulation appears to have grown out of two principal concerns. First, that the airwaves through which radio were broadcast were a finite resource and so needed some sort of control over their allocation and, second, that radio was such a potentially important and influential medium that there should be some control exercised over what was broadcast and by whom. The sheer importance of radio to so many different players and agencies is stressed by Hilmes in her account of pre-war US radio. Radio was at the heart of the transformation of American culture in the 20th century and if anything the intervention of the state added to its significance:

> The creation of the institution of radio broadcasting as a government-regulated extension of the public sphere gave the experience of 'listening-in' more weight and influence than going to the movies or reading a popular magazine; its status as a semipublic institution charged with tasks of education and cultural uplift put it on a par with other official institutions, such as schools, churches, and the government itself. (Hilmes, 1997: 6)

In Britain the acute sense of the importance of radio was expressed in the ideas and policies of John Reith, the first Director General of the BBC, and his formulation of 'public service broadcasting'. Radio was not just the wireless communication of entertainment and information but a 'public service as a cultural, moral and educative force for the improvement of knowledge, taste and manners' and if that was not enough, in addition it would 'bring together all classes of the population' and 'had an immense potential for helping in the creation of an informed and enlightened democracy' (Scannell and Cardiff, 1991: 7). Little wonder then that in the UK radio was fully institutionalised by becoming a national body (a public 'corporation') licensed by parliament, subject to and paid for by a form of tax (the licence fee) and also subject to both parliament-approved 'charter renewal' and regular committees of inquiry. In the USA, regulation took the form of 'consensus broadcasting' in which large, independent radio 'networks' were attentive to government wishes while making assumptions about audience needs (Hilmes, 1997: 7). The day-to-day business of allocating wavelength was the responsibility of the Federal Radio Commission (1927–1934) and then the Federal Communications Commission (FCC).

The history of the FCC is a fascinating account of changing cultural attitudes in the USA. Pre-war regulation acknowledged growing public concern about the power of the networks (NBC, CBS and ABC).

This extended to concern about cross-media ownership: in 1939, two-thirds of the American public got their news from radio and one-third of all stations were owned by newspapers. Given the rise of the Nazi propaganda machine in Germany there were understandable concerns about the concentration of media ownership at the time. Another feature of FCC regulation was a series of policy guidelines called the 'Fairness Doctrine', which encouraged stations to cover political issues and at the same time represent different opinions on those issues. From the 1920s to the heyday of deregulation in the late 1980s, the controversial Fairness Doctrine was used to encourage public debate while maintaining balance in that coverage. The FCC's attempt to regulate balance and fairness in radio political coverage included the highly interventionist 'personal attack' rules which stated that someone attacked on radio had to be notified of the attack and the radio station 'was required to provide a script, tape, or accurate summary of the attack and offer a reasonable opportunity for the attacked person to respond over the same station at no charge' (Kang, 2004: 564). It is interesting to note that the debates in the USA about balance and fairness and how this was to be achieved mirror the same discussions in the BBC about the problem of 'impartiality'. Anxieties about what exactly balance meant and whether the time given to one political party or view should be the same as for the opposition existed on both sides of the Atlantic.

Regulation has not only been about spectrum allocation and political coverage, it has also attempted to prevent the broadcast of sexually explicit material. The famously lewd and sexually provocative Hollywood star Mae West, whose one-liners fizzed with innuendo, made her one and only appearance on NBCs *The Chase and Sandborn Hour* in December 1937. A sketch in which West played a disenchanted Eve was 'laden with innuendo, the Garden of Eden skit emphasised women's desire for carnal experience and Eve's active enthusiasm in relinquishing her virginity for pleasurable purposes' (Murray, 2002: 137). As a result of the furore which followed, mainly from religious groups, NBC declared that West was an 'unfit radio personality' and she did not appear on radio again for 12 years. This was regulation imposed by the broadcaster itself without the need for FCC intervention and there was real concern from some quarters of the American public that radio was in danger of being sanitised: hundreds of letters were written to the FCC in support of Mae West and radio's right to be provocative (Murray, 2002: 138).

British commercial radio began in 1973 and was immediately subject to interventionist regulation by the Independent Broadcasting Authority (IBA). The regulator insisted that the new commercial stations provide balanced information, education, entertainment, high standards, accuracy in news, impartiality and 'the avoidance of offence to good taste and decency' (IBA, 1989: 3). Even as these quite draconian requirements were introduced the winds of change were blowing against state intervention in radio and broadcasting more generally. From the mid-1970s, free market or 'neo-liberal' policies were taking hold in the UK and the USA and the election of Margaret Thatcher as Prime Minister in 1979 and Ronald Reagan as President in 1980 heralded the end of state regulation as it had been known.

In Britain, the Broadcasting Act (1990) led to the lifting of restrictions on ownership and programme content and diversity. Quite quickly, large multi-station radio companies emerged having bought up small local stations and imposed increasingly uniform, networked and highly formatted radio on the audience. No longer restricted by regulations demanding localness and variety of content it proved easy for a company like Great Western Radio (GWR) to acquire over 30 stations and then merge with the Capital Radio Group to form GCap Media. Similarly, the 1980s in the USA saw increasing deregulation as local ownership rules and localism requirements were gradually removed. The Telecommunications Act 1996 saw the end of anti-monopoly rules and restrictions on radio station ownership, originally designed to prevent the dangers of broadcasting monopolies. Within two years of the act being passed, 4000 of the 11,000 radio stations in the USA had been sold. Unprecedented consolidation in the radio industry took place, which has nearly crushed diversity and localism in a once highly diverse industry:

> While deregulation has allowed Clear Channel Communications Inc. to buy up struggling radio stations across the country, the new owners have often pursued profitability by slashing costs, rather than seeking to lure listeners with unique content. As a result, local airwaves are often dominated by a handful of companies that offer a portfolio of similar-sounding radio stations. (Andy Sullivan, in Hilliard and Keith, 2005: 73)

So although regulation had been, at times, obstructive and bureaucratic in its efforts to restrict ownership and imbalance in broadcasting, its removal meant that radio fell into the hands of a very few companies (with a tendency towards one set of political beliefs).

Another impact of deregulation in the USA was the relaxing of rules on fairness and obscenity. In 1987, to be precise, the FCC announced it was no longer enforcing the Fairness Doctrine and as a result the shock jocks of **talk radio** could preach a largely anti-liberal and right-wing message without any need for 'balance'. Howard Stern was particularly outrageous in his attacks on 'welfare queens' and 'bleeding heart' liberals. Although anti-government and anti-immigrant, Stern was a much more contradictory and complex character than he might first appear (Douglas: 1999, 302–9). His libertarianism and determination to break taboos did get him into trouble with the FCC but he then recreated his persona as the crusader for the First Amendment against federal authority. Deregulation, in combination with a more aggressive radio marketplace and the opportunities to sell programmes created by satellite, produced talk radio. As Douglas points out, the participatory ethos of talk radio, the sense of challenging the centres of power, was, ironically, partly the result of the deregulation and consolidation of media ownership in very few hands: 'Populism and participation were the public faces of radio; they masked increased economic concentration and heightened barriers to entry for all but the very rich in the industry itself' (1999: 293).

I am conscious in this survey of radio regulation that there is so much that has been left out. The subject is huge and seems to go to the heart of the business of radio itself. There is room just to mention one other issue that is important for an understanding of regulation. The history of radio includes endless examples of the role of the radio outsider, the amateur: 'DXer', 'sans-filistes', 'pirate', all terms used to describe those who produce and broadcast but are outside the institutions of legal broadcasting (see the entry on **Pirate Radio**). In the USA, the 'little boys in short trousers' before and after the First World War and in the very early 1920s eventually had to give way to licensed and regulated radio stations. In France, the radio fans (or 'sans-filistes') managed to keep going right into the mid-1930s. It has of course been the role of the radio regulator to drive the pirates and amateurs of radio off the airwaves but in recent years this role has been supplemented by some kind of deathbed change of heart. In the USA and the UK regulators have offered community groups the prospect of small-scale broadcasting. In America the FCC gave way to community pressure to allow a greater diversity of voices in the wasteland of post-1996 commercial radio by initiating Low Power FM licences for under-represented social groups. Perhaps a more encouraging, example, however, has been the Radio

Authority initiative to create **Community Radio** stations throughout the UK (a policy then enacted by the next regulator, Ofcom). Like the FCC, the British regulators have been stimulated to create a 'third tier' of radio because of the homogenisation imposed on commercial radio by the conglomerates. Evidence that regulation is not necessarily simply about limiting opportunities but, arguably, can be the agent for stimulating a richness and diversity that the marketplace does not. For radio producers and students, the argument between regulation and unrestricted **commercialism** will no doubt continue to be the source of a debate that goes to the very core of the medium.

FURTHER READING

There are references to radio regulation throughout Hilmes' (1977) history of pre-war American radio. Kang (2004) provides a welcome discussion of the Fairness Doctrine and Murray's (2002) historical account of 'depravity' in Golden Age radio is a useful case study. More recently, Hilliard and Keith (2005) lament the deregulation of American radio. For recent developments see the web sites of the regulators (in the case of the UK, http://www.ofcom.org.uk).

Transmission

> *Radio waves are sent from a transmitter to radio receivers using allotted frequencies in the electromagnetic spectrum.*

The history, and present state, of radio is bound up with the technological fact of transmission. Today, at least in the UK, there is an active debate about the development of digital radio and digital broadcasting. Will the commonly used FM service be replaced by digital radio on one of a number of platforms; digital TV, the Internet or Digital Audio Broadcasting (DAB)? The question of how radio is transmitted and also how and where it is received (on a computer, or a radio receiver, in a car or on a mobile or cell phone) is very important for the continued success of radio as a medium.

Analogue radio uses different frequencies across the available spectrum. For non-specialists (including the author of this book) the technical aspect of radio transmission is largely beyond our comprehension. Precisely how speech in the studio is turned into a radio wave, beamed across the airwaves to the receiving radio set and then turned back into speech was a mystery and a wonder to many when it was invented and remains a mystery to most of us today. There are some basic facts, however, which need to be understood to make sense of a technology that has shaped the development of radio. There are three main frequencies used in analogue (or non-digital) radio; AM (amplitude modulation), FM (frequency modulation) and short wave. In the UK, medium wave and long wave are variations of AM. As a very broad generalisation, AM was the dominant type of radio in the 50 years or so of its history, to be gradually replaced by FM from the 1960s.

Which leaves the case of short wave, a minority form of radio but interesting nonetheless. In the early part of the last century the radio amateurs (or 'DXers' as they were known) were banished by the American regulator to what were thought to be the useless higher frequencies. It turned out, however, that at higher frequencies it was possible to hear sound transmitted from other parts of the world. As Marconi had discovered at the beginning of the century, short wave radio signals bounce off the underside of the ionosphere, between 50 and 100 miles above the earth. This made it possible for DXers to listen to other enthusiasts from around the world. The ability of short wave to broadcast transcontinentally has attracted it to governments wanting to use it for propaganda purposes. After the Second World War, for example, Britain, America and Russia all had international services using short wave and benefiting from its ability to transmit to a selected geographical location and so target the message to that population. Even today the BBC World Service and Radio Moscow both still have short wave services but greatly reduced in favour of other frequencies and platforms.

By 1940 in the USA there were approximately 600 radio stations, all on AM, and about a dozen stations in most large cities with one or two in smaller towns. The quality of AM is particularly poor at night and for most of rural America there was no night-time radio service (Kelly Huff and Sterling, 2004: 84). This status quo was about to be challenged by the arrival of radio using very high frequencies (VHF), more commonly referred to as FM radio (for frequency modulation). The technology for FM transmission had been developed during the 1930s in the USA. Unlike AM or short wave, FM transmission is 'line of sight' between the transmitting mast and the receiver. Because of the curved surface of the earth this limits FM transmission to a maximum of about 65 miles, depending on the terrain and the height of the mast (Sterling, 2004b: 602). But the great advantage of FM is the quality of sound and the absence of any interference, day or night. It took a while for the precise qualities of FM to be fully exploited; the excellent sound quality (especially if the receiver is good) and the ability to broadcast to a local area. The range of FM radio can be manipulated by altering the power of the transmitter. A 100,000-watt transmitter can reach an area with a radius of 65 miles; 50,000 watts reaches 45 miles and 3000 watts, 15 miles. Lower power transmitters, right down to one watt, can broadcast to a single housing block (see the entry on **Micro Radio**). The potential lay in the technology for local or community radio but this was not realised till the 1960s.

The first 15 FM stations began in the USA in 1940 and by 1942 there were 400,000 radio sets capable of receiving the FM signal. In 1945, FM was moved to the frequencies used today; which rendered any FM-only sets obsolete but made the expansion of FM possible. The take-up of FM frequencies was rapid post-war but it was mainly used for simulcasting AM stations (broadcasting the same programming on both AM and FM at the same time). FM-only stations struggled to attract advertisers and the widespread use of simulcasting discouraged consumers from buying FM-only radio sets; FM in 1950s America was in the doldrums. What changed this was partly what Douglas calls the marriage of FM and rock (1999: 275). In the counter culture of the 1960s, FM was the frequency of choice for the progressive rock stations with their extremely laid back DJs using a style called 'free form' FM (Douglas, 1999: 13). One of the reasons Douglas offers for the enthusiastic adoption of FM by the counter-culture was their use of mind-expanding drugs, 'the use of marijuana and psychedelics increased the appreciation of and demand for improved clarity and richness in sound reproduction' (1999: 269).

In Britain the BBC was also slow to develop the new FM technology. By 1960, however, there were 20 FM transmitters (Street, 2002: 105), even if the public was reluctant to pay the price for FM receivers. In both the USA and the UK the growth of music radio, and especially rock and pop music, combined with the gradually falling price of FM receivers (increasingly in small portable transistor radios), contributed to the rise of FM radio. In the UK both BBC local radio and, from 1973, commercial radio, simulcasted on AM and FM and so FM's ability to reach a local audience was exploited. By 1979 in the USA, FM surpassed AM in audience size and increasingly AM frequencies became the home of news and talk radio.

In Britain, digital radio was introduced in the mid-1990s across a range of platforms; digital television, on the Internet and, using VHF frequencies, on Digital Audio Broadcasting (DAB). The BBC launched digital radio, carrying all its existing services, in 1995 (Street, 2002: 131), an 'historic moment' in the opinion of the Managing Director of BBC Radio:

> ... the dawn of a third age of radio – the technological progression from AM, which is now 100 years old, and FM, now 50 years old, into the digital multi-media world of the 21st century. Consumers will get superb quality sound, a fade-free signal and a whole range of new services on simple, easy-to-use sets. (Quoted in Street, 2002: 131)

At the time of writing the price of the DAB set in the UK has fallen significantly and there has been steady growth in the size of the audience listening to DAB services. The BBC remains firmly behind the development of DAB in Britain providing digital-only services like the music station, 6 Music. The BBC and the regulator, Ofcom, envisage the eventual switch off of analogue radio, although commercial broadcasters, not benefiting from licence fee income, are more sceptical. Digital radio, although backed by some powerful institutions, may itself be increasingly undermined by the next generation of transmission technologies, portable Internet receivers using wireless technology. As larger areas of towns and cities are able to receive the Internet through wireless connections so Internet radio becomes a genuine alternative to both FM and DAB (see the entry on **Convergence**).

FURTHER READING

Street (2002) charts the development of radio technology in his concise history of radio in Britain. There are some excellent summaries of transmission technology in the separate entries on AM, FM and short wave in Sterling (2004a). Douglas dedicates a chapter to 'the FM revolution' (1999: 256–83).

Part IV
Politics and the
Public Sphere

Current Affairs

> **Current affairs is a speech radio genre that provides comment and analysis on the news.**

The term 'current affairs' is mainly associated with British rather than US broadcasting. American radio and television has traditionally seen news and comment on the news (or 'news analysis') as one and the same. In the context of the British media it is usually possible to distinguish between news and current affairs (although these may be combined, for example in radio 'news magazines') and also to distinguish between the more analytical and news related approach of current affairs and documentary (see the separate entries on **Documentaries and Features**). The British television producer Jeremy Isaacs has summed the distinction between news and current affairs with particular clarity, 'If the job of a news service was to tell us what was happening at any given moment, then the job of current affairs was to help us understand what was happening' (quoted in Holland, 2006: xii). In her discussion of 1950s factual television, Thumin comments that documentary 'is a more straightforward generic descriptor than current affairs' noting also the 'generic fluidity' of current affairs (2004: 44). She also refers to the distinction between 'hard' and 'soft' versions with the former being mainly concerned with politics, economics and foreign affairs and the latter straying into 'soft' issues including marriage, health, crime, consumer matters and even celebrities and show business.

In the UK, a distinction between the 'facts' of news and the 'opinions' of current affairs can be traced back to organisational divisions in the early BBC. The first manager and Director General of the BBC, John Reith, had to battle with the government of the day to allow the BBC to broadcast anything about matters of 'controversy'. Perhaps understandably, there was some anxiety about the intervention of radio, that new and almost magical medium, into the world of politics. In 1928, however, the ban was partially lifted and the BBC was allowed to cover political issues of the day.

Defining current affairs is not an easy task. A great deal of what we would consider news contains implied or explicit comment. At the same time, documentaries and features may also include comment on the news. But in the British case there was an early concern about combining news and comment, which in the 1930s was provided through the medium of the radio 'talk'. This concern, which led in 1935 to the creation of separate News and Talks departments in the BBC (and therefore the separation of news from comment) was the result of the suspicion that comment or analysis might somehow contaminate the purity of news facts and as a result harm the standing of the BBC. As Scannell and Cardiff put it, 'the newspapers saw the separation of News from Talks as the BBC's "Answer to Tory [Conservative Party] suspicions of radicalism" (1991: 118). In reality the 1930s 'topical talk' rarely dealt with political issues in anything but the most cautious manner. There was particular nervousness within the BBC that talks dealing with the growing international crisis would offend its political masters and the treatment of unemployment, one of the main features of Scannell and Cardiff's history of the period, tended to moralise rather than critically examine the causes of the problem.

Current affairs as an identifiably separate broadcasting genre emerged after the Second World War in a much less deferential Britain and one where there seemed to be an increased hunger for both news and comment. In the case of television, pioneers like Grace Wyndham Goldie at the BBC launched a number of eminent examples of the genre including the BBC's 'flagship' current affairs programme, *Panorama*, and ITV's *World in Action* and *This Week*. As Holland points out, the role of television current affairs was not just to respond to what she calls 'the desire to understand' but also to promote democratic engagement, to act as an 'angry buzz' in the ear of the British establishment (2006: xiii). For students of radio there are important lessons to be learned from the example of television current affairs. There clearly are similarities between the television and radio versions of the genre; the use of in-depth political interviews, of journalists reporting on location, studio discussions, the presence of an 'anchor' or guiding presenter, all of these can be found in examples of radio and television current affairs. Towards the end of the 20th century, however, the television version seemed to be in terminal decline whereas the evidence from radio was much more encouraging.

In their evocatively titled report for the Campaign for Quality Television, *A Shrinking Iceberg Travelling South*, Barnett and Seymour sum up what they see as the perilous state of British television current affairs. Having noted the more caution and less experimentation in television drama they state:

In current affairs, this translates into more emphasis on the domestic, consumer and ratings-friendly subjects at the expense of covering foreign affairs, Northern Ireland or more complex political and economic issues. It also favours a more emotional or picture-led approach to current affairs at the expense of more analytical or investigative programmes ... there is a deep-rooted sense of crisis about this television genre. (1999: 5)

They also bemoan the decline in 'hard' current affairs which they define as 'political, industrial and foreign stories.' In a similar vein, Holland refers to the 'virtual abandonment' of traditional current affairs in her book which charts the rise and final end of ITV's *This Week*.

What, then, of radio? In a particularly interesting discussion of the virtues of BBC Radio 4's 'intellectualism', Crisell argues that in covering and analysing the news, radio has a distinct advantage in being (to use his term) 'blind' (2004: 9). Because radio current affairs relies on language it cannot use pictures of the events being discussed. For Crisell this is an advantage because 'radio is, potentially at least, a much more "intellectual" medium than television, whose words are often overwhelmed by its images'. Images are misleading (he uses the endlessly repeated image of the planes crashing into the Twin Towers on 11 September 2001) because they evoke an emotional or irrational response. So it may be that this theoretical advantage, radio's comparative freedom from the diverting clutter of visual images, has allowed radio current affairs to survive.

A notable survivor, and arguably the single most important current affairs programme in British broadcasting, radio or television, is BBC Radio 4's *Today*. Starting as a rather 'light' magazine programme for 'people on the move' in 1957, it was originally envisaged that this 'morning miscellany' would include reviews of plays and records, dress and fashion items, weather notes, personal stories as well as more serious industrial and foreign items. In his history of the first 40 years of *Today*, Donovan describes its development through a period of slightly eccentric presentation in the 1960s and on to its pre-eminent position as 'the indispensable alarm clock of the elite, a three-line whip for the ears of all those interested or involved in public life' (1998: 192). More recently the main presenter of this three-hour news and current affairs magazine, John Humphrys has used the 20-minute interview, always starting at 8.10 a.m., to grill politicians in his famously 'macho' style. There can be little doubt that *Today* is a very important and influential provider of both news and comment, without transgressing the rules which forbid the BBC to appear to 'editorialise' as a newspaper might do.

Radio current affairs also survives on the BBC in programmes like the intellectually demanding, single subject *Analysis* and the survey of reflections from around the world *From Our Own Correspondent*. Radio current affairs, as we noted at the beginning of this entry, is not always easy to identify. The 'generic boundaries' can be uncertain and it is clear that the listener's understanding of political issues can be enhanced by good news or current affairs programmes as well as phone-ins, documentaries and even more experimental programming. Moore has examined the role of the BBC Northern Ireland radio service, BBC Radio Ulster and its engagement with the political situation in Northern Ireland in the late 1990s: 'For most people in Northern Ireland ... it is not television but radio that plays the greatest role in contributing to political and cultural values (2003: 88). The station has a conventional morning current affairs programme, *Good Morning Ulster*, and also a phone-in programme, *Talkback*, which allows for the expression of quite extreme sectarian views characteristic of the province at the time. Of particular interest is Radio Ulster's *Legacy* series which ran daily for the whole of 1999 and featured the two-minute testimonies of those caught up in Northern Ireland's infamous 'troubles'. It would be hard to define such as programme as current affairs but equally hard to deny that it contributed to understanding and even to political change:

> Legacy shows a corporation still seeking ways to approach broadcasting in a divided society ... The pieces were broadcast at a time when the negotiations around the progress of the Good Friday Agreement were particularly intense. Any intervention in a political sense by the BBC would have been both difficult and controversial. Legacy encouraged listeners to confront the sometimes unpalatable facts of sectarian violence and this confrontation made violence the central issue of debate. (Moore, 2003: 99)

Radio current affairs continues to be an important part of BBC output, especially on Radio 4 but also on the news and sport service 5 Live. As Moore shows, it can adapt to become something quite different from the standard magazine format of *Today* (although that example continues to flourish) and this need for flexibility, introducing the voice of the 'ordinary' person, may be a necessary part of its survival.

FURTHER READING

There is a striking lack of introductory literature on current affairs radio although Crisell (2004: 3–19) and Shingler and Wieringa (1998: 45–7) provide general introductory observations. There are, however, some interesting sources on specific current affairs programmes including Donovan (1998) on the *Today* programme, Moore (2003) on *Legacy* and references throughout Hendy's history of BBC Radio 4 (2007).

Development

> *Development usually refers to the improvement in the economic health of a country. It can be helped by the use of radio for education and information.*

There is plenty of evidence that radio can contribute to improving the health, education and general well-being of people in the poorest parts of the world. Africa is a particularly important example of the 'development' potential of radio for a variety of reasons. Radio reaches more people in Africa than any other medium, more than television or the press (Mytton, 2004: 17). It is particularly influential in sub-Saharan Africa where the success and importance of radio is due to a number of different factors. It is much cheaper and more portable than television and does not rely on a regular supply of mains electricity: the television industry is also far less developed in Africa than in other parts of the world. In addition, high levels of illiteracy in parts of Africa contribute to radio's popularity over the press as does the prevalence of orally-based cultures. Although radio plays an important part in development in other parts of the world this entry will focus on the case of Africa.

Radio began in Africa during the pre-war colonial period when it was largely a tool of the colonial power. Broadcasters like the South Africa Broadcasting Company were based on a BBC model although it was common for broadcasters to come increasingly under government control (Mytton, 2004: 17). There are a variety of different categories of radio station in Africa today including state-run stations, propaganda stations owned by politicians, purely commercial music-based stations and, particularly important for the theme of development, community stations. The latter often use low-power FM, are run by local volunteers and partly financed by churches or non-governmental organisations.

Organisations such as UNESCO, the UN and the British charity Oxfam, as well as the Catholic church, all fund **community radio** stations in Africa.

The sort of issues addressed on development-oriented radio include health awareness, and especially HIV/AIDS, the importance of education, improving the role of women and advice for farmers. In her case study of a community station in Mali, West Africa, Mary Myers refers to local broadcasters as 'the mid-wives of rural self expression', allowing people in the local community to express themselves (2000: 95). The presenters included a farmer and a nurse and they spoke in the local language, unlike on state-run radio where broadcasters were often civil servants speaking in French and extending government policy to the masses. In community radio stations such as Daande Duwansa listeners often knew the presenters and many had family ties with them. The station stressed the importance of food hygiene, among its many development themes, encouraged girls to go to school and also tried to raise awareness about the dangers and consequences of female circumcision.

Mozambique is one of the poorest countries in the world and has endured some 30 years of civil war which has seriously damaged its infrastructure. The first community radio station went on air in 1994 and by 2005 there were 50 (Jallov, 2005: 21). In her 'impact assessment' of community radio, Jallov stresses the importance of giving value to a local community and thereby building up self-confidence. She also describes the emphasis on HIV/AIDS, encouraging respect for youths and women and in cholera prevention:

> ... community radio stations can become efficient local knowledge centres which empower communities by reinforcing existing local capacity and changing the local dynamics in a democratic direction. Community radio can help uncover experience and knowledge previously not visible, and provide a space and voice for communities previously marginalized from public life, including women. The radio station furthermore functions as the local technological centre, in most places providing access to telephones, faxes and photocopiers. (2005: 33)

The Kenyan Broadcasting Company's weekly drama programme *Radio Theatre* provides a different example of 'development radio' much more in tune with public service models of broadcasting. This is government-sponsored radio spreading messages of development, peace and unity and 'to this end, out of the 54 plays produced per year, quite a large percentage of them have been used to foster images of development and progress against backward and retrogressive cultures' (Ligaga, 2005: 109). In the play *Not Now* broadcast in 2003 (see also the entry on **Drama**), a girl is about to be forced into marriage and to become the fourth wife of an old man. She escapes and manages to return to school and goes on to get a job. A story of everyday life is used to promote development themes of education and employment for women and against traditional marriage practices.

FURTHER READING

The collection of essays on African broadcast cultures edited by Fardon and Furniss (2000) is an excellent starting point for further reading and the chapters by Mytton (2000) and Myers (2000) are particularly recommended. More recently, articles in *The Radio Journal* by Jallov (2005) and Ligaga (2005) are both very readable and informative.

Gender

> *Gender is used to refer to the cultural differences between men and women and in the case of radio to male and female producers and audiences and to programming targeted at either men or women.*

There are a number of good reasons for seeing a special relationship between radio and women. For thinking that more than any other mass media, radio articulates women's experiences and feelings. Looking at radio programming and genres and evidence of the expression of women's experiences and concerns tends to reinforce this idea. In addition, some of the most influential radio innovators have been women. A very different approach, however, can be taken which sees radio (both production and content) as predominantly masculine. Radio can, for example, be seen as absolutely central to the development of masculinity: as Douglas puts it in her history of American radio, it played a key role in 'tuning and retuning certain visions of manhood' (Douglas, 1999: 14).

There are some particularly graphic and interesting examples of radio's gendered identity, mainly from radio's historical past, but before we consider those it might be worth thinking a bit about the nature of gender and the social roles of men and women. At the time of the birth of radio in the 1920s, social roles based on gender (and for that matter also on race) were highly segregated. Women's place was in the home and in Britain and America women were largely segregated from the workplace. 'Women's issues' were clearly defined as domestic and familial and women were frequently depicted as hysterical, weak and vulnerable. This gendered social division was challenged throughout the 20th century by feminism and partly eroded by the upheavals of the two world wars. Most commentators agree that in the 1960s increased liberalism in social attitudes to gender, race and sexuality not only helped to empower women but also challenged traditional notions of masculinity. So what has this got to do with radio? To put it simply, programmes which were once seen as 'women's radio', for example day-time magazines with items about cooking and children, may appeal to men today far more than they did to their fathers. Similarly, sports programmes, once seen as the reserve of men and boys, are increasingly presented by women and might even attract a female audience.

Histories of the development of radio in the 1920s and 1930s provide a useful way of understanding the gendered nature of the medium. In the USA after the end of the First World War there was a particularly active community of radio amateurs. Before the establishment of the powerful radio networks and the system of radio regulation, and while radio technology was still in its infancy, the airwaves were the plaything of largely male amateurs. Similarly, in France in the 1920s there were large numbers of 'sans-filistes' ('radio fans') organised in clubs who both listened and broadcast in the period before and even after the arrival of formalised broadcasting (Street, 2006a: 267). The main amateur activity in the USA was 'DXing' or seeing what range of listening could be achieved on the primitive crystal radio sets. Books and magazines flourished to support the amateurs with revealing titles like *The Radio Boys* and *The Wireless Man*. Soon, however, radio made the move from the garage to the living room and in doing that revealed its potential as a medium for women as well as men.

A useful way of thinking about radio and gender is to contrast the masculine public sphere, the world of politics and commerce, with the private sphere, the world of emotions and family life, traditionally seen as feminine. If we accept that this division existed in the early part of the 20th century then the introduction of radio into the home made a feminine intervention into the public sphere a possibility. As Lacey argues in her examination of radio in Germany before the Nazi period women began to find a public voice which imitated private female discourse (Lacey, 2000). She suggests that radio which allowed 'chit-chat', gossip and 'heart-to-heart' communication revolutionised women's experience in the home. All German radio stations used women's voices to speak to women in their role as housewives and mothers.

It was the introduction of drama serials (or 'soaps') which really made women's experiences a public event. The American broadcaster Irna Phillips produced one of the first day-time soaps, *Painted Dreams*, from the Chicago station WGN in 1930. Hilmes sees the day-time serial as part of a feminine opposition or counter to the male public sphere:

> Arguably, female writers and producers such as Phillips opened up a space on the public airwaves for a feminine subaltern counterpublic to emerge, who responded to the serials' attempts to open up the restricted sphere of public discussion to topics usually dismissed as 'women's issues' – private, personal and therefore unsuited to public discourse. (1997: 160)

The extent of this largely pre-war phenomenon was huge. In 1936 in the USA, 55 per cent of daytime radio consisted of serial dramas which featured largely female casts and were mainly about women's experiences (see the entry on **Soaps**).

This is not to say that examples of radio for women were liberating or challenged male domination in society as a whole. Bored, lonely housewives listening to DJs in the 1960s may have taken pleasure from their romantic visitors but did so in terms of orthodox heterosexuality. Rather like the women readers of romantic fiction, women's pleasure in music radio was a 'declaration of independence' but one which reinforced patriarchal relationships (Radway, 1987). One of the most evocative explorations of the two-faced nature of radio for women is to be found in the work of Susan Douglas (1994). She describes her own experiences of growing up in the USA in the late 1950s and early 1960s. Girl bands like the Chiffons and the Shangri-Las sang about love and sex, about female sexuality and rebellion.

> This music was, simultaneously, deeply personal and highly public, fusing our neurotic, quivering inner selves with the neurotic, quivering inner selves of others...

gender

We listened to this music in the darkness of our bedrooms, driving around in our parents' cars, on the beach, making out with some boy... (Douglas, 1994: 87)

The songs that Douglas and her friends listened to 'were about both escaping from and yet acquiescing to the demands of a male-dominated society' (1994: 90).

What of the male experience of radio? One way of answering that question is to look at sport on radio. In Britain, the BBC used sports coverage to build up the calendar of events which both marked the year and reinforced the central cultural role of the corporation. The Boat Race, major horse races, football, rugby, tennis at Wimbledon and cricket all played their part in reinforcing the BBC's significance by admitting millions of listeners to these essentially national events. In America, baseball and boxing brought the intensely masculine world of professional and amateur sport right into the bedroom and living room and expressed traditionally masculine values of toughness, competition and aggression. Twenty-five million listened to the 1942 World Series and sports reporting produced the 'masculine skill' of wordplay (Douglas, 1999). British radio in the 1990s witnessed the creation of two national sports-focused radio stations, BBC Radio 5 Live and the commercial station talkSPORT. So male in its appeal has 5 Live been that it is universally referred to as 'Radio Bloke' (Starkey, 2004b). The endless chat about football, largely between men, has unsurprisingly resulted in a predominantly male audience.

As the pre-war soaps can be described as among the most feminised areas of radio programming, so US **talk radio** from the 1980s was the site of a blatant masculinity. The much discussed degradation of the public sphere in the 20th century, its so called 'refeudalisation' as a result of the growth of media power (Habermas, 1989) created a space which men like Howard Stern and Dom Imus were happy to occupy. Politics in the mainstream had become slick, superficial and dead and the arrogant rantings of talk radio hosts created much more exciting electronic surrogates for the town hall. Stern was obsessed with sex, a 'mouthy arrogant stud' (Douglas, 1999: 304). This was the celebration of the locker room; according to Dinitia Smith listening to Dom Imus was like 'being stuck in a classroom with a bunch of prepubescent boys while the teacher is out of the room. Imus lets the educated male who grew up in the 1960s and was taught not to judge women simply by the size of their breasts to be, for one glorious moment of his day, an unreconstructed chauvinist pig' (Douglas,

1994: 306). But even in the male world of talk radio anxieties about masculinity arise. As Douglas points out, Howard Stern has an insecure and feminised side. He swung between the masculine and the feminine with a persona that was at times both arch conservative but also libertarian. Vulgar and pornographic but also prudish.

Gender and radio are intimately entwined and this entry has only provided a glimpse of a complex and important area of radio studies. Women producers may want to make programmes which speak to other women and the same is sometimes true for men. Types of programming may be identified as 'for women' or 'for men' and appeal to gendered audiences and in this regard radio is much like other mass media. To end on a speculative note, some of radio's qualities, its intimacy, its nostalgia, its ability to address emotions, might encourage the idea that there is something essentially *feminine* about radio.

FURTHER READING

What are arguably the two most important cultural histories of American radio, Hilmes (1997) and Douglas (1999), are both written by feminists and both include substantial analysis of the position of women as producers and the audience. Women and British radio is the subject of an excellent collection of very readable and interesting articles (Mitchell, 2000).

Hate Radio

> *Hate radio is radio on which messages of hate towards a social group are broadcast with the aim of encouraging acts of violence towards them.*

Radio, like any mass medium, has the potential to be democratic as well as propagandist. Radio has been seized on by governments, both democratic and totalitarian, to tell lies and distortions to listeners (see the entry on **Propaganda**). The phenomenon of hate radio, however, is not the same as simple propaganda. This is radio which has the explicit aim of encouraging the listener literally to hate a particular social (usually ethnic) group in society. The narrow definition of hate radio suggested here is further refined by Richard Carver who uses a United Nations definition which includes both hatred and incitement to action:

> The problem of hate speech is a permanently vexing one for defenders of freedom of expression. At a certain point, exercise of free speech begins to impinge on the rights of others – for example, freedom from discrimination – and these rights need to be weighed against each other. After its stirring defence of freedom of expression in Article 19, ICCPR continues in Article 20:
>
> 1.   Any propaganda for war shall be prohibited by law.
>
> 2.   Any advocacy of national, racial or religious hatred that constitutes incitement to discrimination, hostility or violence shall be prohibited by law. (2000: 191)

Searching for cases of radio which are deliberately designed to incite listeners to take action against others fortunately produces few examples. The notorious right-wing Catholic priest Father Charles E. Coughlin attacked minority groups on American radio in the 1930s. He railed against Jews, trade unionists, immigrants and communists, 'Coughlin was the forerunner of the Holocaust-deniers and neo Nazis of today' (Keith and Hilliard, 2004: 694). In the same entry in the *Encyclopedia of Radio*, Keith and Hilliard go on to discuss openly racist talk show hosts like Joe Pine and Bob Grant (who referred to African-Americans as 'savages') without going so far as to include the more recent shock jocks like Howard Stern and Don Imus. The latter may have hateful and even hate-filled things to say but it would be a step too far to see them as motivated by a desire to foment violence. The 1990s in America saw the rise of hate radio on some small AM stations as various right-wing extremists, white supremacists, neo-Nazis, survivalists and conspiracy theorists took to the air in a short period of time before the Internet became their natural home.

By far the most important example of hate radio has been the case of Radio-Télévision Libre des Mille Collines (RTLM) in Rwanda. The station was launched in July 1993 and began encouraging Hutus to murder Tutsis the following April. Almost one million Tutsis died in the Rwandan genocide. There is some disagreement about the exact role and influence of RTLM. Research by Kellow and Steeves is adamant that years of racist radio propaganda had exerted a huge influence over the largely illiterate population and had been largely responsible for the mass killings (Hendy 2000: 202). Because the population had learned to trust radio they were completely uncritical of it and the Hutu population simply did what they were told. A rather more cautious approach is taken by Carver who shesses the very late start of RTLM's murderous instructions. He argues that the role of hate radio in Rwanda has been exaggerated and that there is no proof that the admittedly genocidal broadcasts actually made people commit murder (Carver, 2000: 190). There are other examples of hate radio in Africa including Radio Pretoria, a neo-Nazi Afrikaner station in 1994, and state-owned radio in Zaire in the early 1990s.

In Sydney, Australia in 2006 there were running battles between white Australian gangs and Middle Eastern youths. The fighting had been sparked by rumours of attacks on lifeguards by largely Lebanese young men. A study of the role of radio in the disturbances by Catharine Lumby shows that even Sydney's popular 2GB station was contributing to the violence with presenters referring to Lebanese youths as 'mongrels' and 'vicious and cowardly' (*The Guardian*, Saturday 21 October 2006). Radio presenters encouraged whites to believe that they were under attack and that the police were ineffective. Whether or not this counts as hate radio is a matter of interpretation but this example underlines the problem of distinguishing between the sadly not uncommon racism of talk radio and the rarer incitement of hate radio.

FURTHER READING

There are two useful introductory texts which discuss the phenomenon; Hendy (2000: 200–4) incorporates research on the Rwandan case and Keith and Hilliard (2004) are very informative about the American examples. For a more detailed and critical evaluation see Carver (2000).

hate radio

Journalism

> *Journalism refers to the practice of the radio reporter in gathering and presenting news and comment.*

Radio journalism is not fundamentally different from news gathering in other media; in fact many journalists write for newspapers as well as working for either radio or television, or both. The age of the multimedia journalist has arrived and the Internet has played an important part in this convergence. There are, however, differences in the nature of, for example, an article in a paper and a radio journalist's report and the particular properties of radio journalism have evolved over time. Some of the issues here are developed in the entry on **News**.

In the BBC there was little systematic radio reporting before the Second World War. Most news was provided by the news agencies and by 1939 there were only two dedicated BBC radio journalists. Remarkably, there was no BBC journalist in Spain to report the civil war, which had begun in 1936, until the end of the conflict in 1939 (Nicholas, 1996: 191). But the Second World War, after an initial period of inertia and censorship, revolutionised radio news reporting in the BBC. Eye-witness reports of battles by BBC reporters were recorded on extremely cumbersome disc recorders. Richard Dimbleby was one of the most famous of these journalists; in January 1943 he recorded a report while on a Lancaster bomber on a raid over Berlin. At the same time, the great American radio journalist Edward R. Murrow was also reporting on the war for audiences back home. Murrow had been in Vienna at the time of the German invasion and then moved to London where he gave his famous reports on the war from the basement of the BBC's Broadcasting House in central London:

> They were timely, compelling and immediate for a world breathlessly awaiting word about the quickly growing war. And each one began with his standard and quite dramatic signature opening: 'This … is London'. (Limburg, 2004: 966)

Although radio journalists may not be a distinct group for the reasons I have already given, the skills needed to provide oral reports are not the same as for television or newspapers. The success of reporters such as Dimbleby and Murrow was their ability to use speech to convey what were often strongly visual events. In the case of radio in the UK different approaches to radio reporting have developed and it is possible to identify these in radio news.

The most traditional approach to radio reporting is the news talk in which a radio journalist (sometimes referred to as a 'correspondent') scripts and then records a short crafted talk. The BBC Radio 4 programme *From Our Own Correspondent* is a weekly compilation of news talks and it illustrates how speech can provide a unique style of reporting, exemplified by the BBC journalist Fergal Keane whose reports on the end of apartheid were both graphic and emotionally charged. A quite different style and approach was developed in commercial radio in the UK which began in 1973. LBC/IRN was in direct competition with BBC news coverage and especially in London. It competed by challenging the BBC's more traditional approach to news, and in particular the failure to introduce the greater use of actuality and eye-witness accounts which became characteristic of commercial radio's news service Independent Radio News (Chignell, 2007). With their own distinctive, lively and populist style of journalism, IRN reporters gave live reports from riots, wars and other dramatic events. Their spontaneous, live reporting was often combined by dramatic actuality.

One of the particular achievements of BBC news has been the development of the political interview. Up to the 1950s, interviews with public figures tended to be deferential in the extreme. As the British tendency to deference and respect for those in positions waned in the late 1950s and early 1960s, a more assertive and combative approach began to develop. Individual BBC journalists became famous for interrogating politicians on news and current affairs programmes, for example, the famously acerbic John Humphrys on BBC Radio 4's *Today* programme. In recent years, however, there is evidence that the news interviews is being replaced by 'two-ways', dialogues *between* radio presenters and reporters:

> Nowadays news programmes of all kinds contain dialogues, which are not interviews with public figures or institutional spokespersons, but rather exchanges with other journalists working for the same organization. Foreign correspondents do not simply file reports, they are interviewed in live two-way satellite links. Routinely, they are invited to speculate about what they have just reported. (Tolson, 2006: 61)

Tolson describes a move away from the probing, in-depth news interview to a situation where the airwaves are increasingly monopolised by broadcasters themselves. The style has become far more informal, even gossipy, and banter and humour are employed to display the 'mutual affiliation' of the reporters or presenters to their news organisation (Tolson, 2006: 68).

One of the most important developments in radio journalism has been the slow but gradual improvement in the employment of women. The traditional image of the journalist was male and even macho; 'hard-bitten, heavy-drinking, unfeeling, objective, cynical workaholics' (Haworth, 2000: 252). New technology used by multi-skilled journalists has encouraged women and removed the largely male workforce of radio technicians. The physically intrusive door-stepping approach to news gathering has declined and at the same time news specifically aimed at women has grown in importance.

FURTHER READING

Fortunately there is a particularly well researched book on international radio news and journalism (Crook, 1998). For an historical view, Nicholas (1996) is excellent on the BBC in the Second World War. Although not strictly about radio, Tolson (2006) provides a good analysis of news talk.

News

> *News refers to the regular reporting of news events on radio, usually an hourly event and featuring scripted news announcements as well as the reports of news journalists.*

The delivery of news is surely a defining feature of radio and one of its most important strengths as it faces competition from audio on demand. Radio news seems to perform a number of different functions apart from simply providing up-to-date information about ongoing events. These are: keeping the audience listening as the news narrative unfolds; emphasising the 'liveness' of the broadcast; reinforcing the co-presence of presenter/listener; and reinforcing national identity in nationwide broadcasts or local identity in local radio. In their discussion of radio news, Shingler and Wieringa suggest that its success is due to our 'audio socialisation' – the gradual process of learning to listen to and trust radio as a source of information (1998: 95). Radio, and perhaps public service radio in particular, has built up a reputation for truth and honesty and for those who see radio as an 'old friend' and experience a sense of intimacy with the medium, news on radio is particularly plausible. If this is true it is probably also true that it was a phenomenon of the last century when generations of listeners were socialised to trust radio, and in particular during wartime.

The history of radio news can be conveniently divided into two periods. In the first, from the 1920s to the Second World War, radio became an authoritative and trusted source of information for citizens of the UK and the USA. In the second period, broadly from the 1960s to the present, it is the rise of audience participation in news which is the main theme.

News and current affairs have become central to the mission and reputation of the BBC (see the entry on **Current Affairs**). In the case of BBC radio, news bulletins are an important part of the music networks and BBC Radio 4 and 5 Live feature news and comment throughout their schedules. But the newly formed British Broadcasting Company (as it was known until 1927) had very little news indeed in 1922. The newspaper owners were understandably worried about competition from radio and used their influence to restrict radio news which could not be broadcast before 7 p.m. and had to be provided by the Reuters news agency. The General Strike of 1926 was a watershed in the development of BBC news and the BBC itself. Because the newspapers stopped printing, radio became the only source of news and showed its ability, while remaining formally independent of government, to be the means of controlling public opinion during the crisis. From the trade union point of view, the BBC was biased against them (and to be any different would probably have been impossible) but in terms of public service broadcasting this was proof that radio could be an indispensable source of information (Scannell and Cardiff, 1991: 32).

In the USA, radio news really came into its own at the outbreak of the Second World War in Europe (1939). Although the USA was neutral at this stage in the hostilities there was intense interest and excitement in American audiences as events unfolded. The US networks had reporters in European capitals and Susan Douglas describes what listeners heard on 13 March 1938 on CBS:

'The program of *St. Louis Blues*, normally scheduled for this time, has been cancelled.' Instead, 'To bring you the picture of Europe tonight, Columbia now presents a special broadcast which will include pickups direct from

London, from Paris, and other capitals in Europe.' His tone was urgent yet conversational. 'Tonight the world trembles, torn by conflicting forces. Throughout this day, event has crowded upon event in tumultuous Austria ... News has flowed across the Atlantic in a steady stream'. (Edward R. Murrow, quoted in Douglas, 1999: 178)

The most famous of these American broadcasters working in Europe was Edward R. Murrow, who broadcast on shortwave during the 'Blitz' as well as flying in a B-17 raid over Berlin and entering Buchenwald concentration camp with Allied troops. Murrow developed radio news reporting with his use of a combination of drama, informality and information. Together with the other US correspondents, Murrow used a conversational and personal style to communicate the unfolding international crisis to US audiences.

The Second World War also acted as a defining moment in the development of the BBC and radio news in the UK. Using new recording equipment it was possible to report directly from the front and keep listeners informed of the progress of the war. The programme *War Report* was broadcast in the last year of the war and BBC reporters, using the new Midget disc recorder, provided vivid accounts of the conflict which were heard within 24 hours of having been recorded (Street, 2006b: 285). Despite the obvious success and importance of radio coverage of the war there were also major deficiencies in both American and British versions of events. The BBC, for example, failed to report the extent of the Holocaust. Crook argues in his history of radio journalism that the failure to report the mass extermination of the Jews resulted in widespread ignorance of the Holocaust in the UK right up to the end of the war in 1945 (Crook, 1999: 202). The situation was partly remedied by the famous report by Richard Dimbleby who entered the Belsen concentration camp with his portable disc recorder in April 1945. His harrowing and moving report at last communicated to British listeners something of the horror of the camps but even this iconic report by one of the BBC's main correspondents was only broadcast after Dimbleby had to threaten to resign unless it was broadcast (Crook, 1999: 202).

By the end of the war, despite its failings, radio had become a recognised and widely trusted source of news and had also developed the personal, conversational style of reporting which could give it a greater intensity and immediacy than newspapers. News became an almost ubiquitous feature of radio and quickly established codes and conventions which have changed little in the last 50 years. The regular news break, often on the hour, has become a universal characteristic of the radio schedule and news presentation frequently conforms to quite rigid expectations:

> The news is usually read by a deep male voice and/or with an authoritative, portentous delivery of the script; and inevitably it is scripted (in contrast with the intimacy and apparent spontaneity of most spoken-word radio). Radio news speech is quite distinctive from other kinds of talk on radio, in part because it makes no or little attempt to disguise that this talk is being read from a written script. The effect is to keep the reader at a distance from the listener, reflecting the 'truth', objectivity and authority of news. (Dunn, 2003: 118)

Another convention of radio news which has grown in recent years, is the habit of news presenters engaging in discussion with reporters. The 'two-way' as this exchange is called is common in news magazines and sequences where there is plenty of time to fill. The presenter can invite the reporter to add colour and comment to a news item and even to speculate about what might happen in the future. Tolson argues that the increased use of two-ways is part of a wider development which includes two presenters discussing the news with each other and with other 'support personnel' in the studio (2006: 70). It could be argued that this is a recognition of the subjective nature of news, that news in fact is not 'truth' but open to negotiation and interpretation (see the entry in **Journalism**).

Another development in radio news, suggested at the beginning of this entry, was the growth of radio news reporting and comment which foregrounded the citizen as commentator and even journalist. I would argue that this development can be traced back to the arrival of television after the Second World War. Television news provided dramatic pictures of events such as the Korean and Vietnam wars which helped to make television the main source of news for most people. If 'post-television' radio was to survive as a news source it would have to introduce new approaches to the reporting of events and one of those approaches was to introduce the voice of the listener.

While radio could not compete with the spectacle of television news, it could pioneer an interactivity in news. In the UK, the radio phone-in as a device for making it possible for people to engage in

news

the news and events more widely was first introduced in BBC local radio at the end of the 1960s but only became a fully-fledged part of the schedule with the introduction of commercial radio in 1973. This allowed listeners to comment on events in a way not possible on television. Once again a war provides an important example of a development in radio news. The Falklands war of 1983 was largely a 'radio war' because television cameras were not allowed with the British forces as they recaptured the islands from the Argentinean invaders. The commercial news provider Independent Radio News did have a reporter on board a British ship and his reports were as avidly listened to as those earlier Second World War reports. However, an interesting feature of radio coverage was the new opportunity for British listeners to phone up their local commercial radio station and join one of the many phone-ins or just listen to what other listeners had to say.

Both radio and television news have benefited from the widespread use of the mobile or cell phone. Armed with mobiles to report events directly to news organisations as they happen the 'citizen journalist' has become a crucial part of the news-gathering machine. For radio this has meant that immediate reports from the scene of events can be broadcast, further enhancing the interactive and listener-friendly quality of radio news. Text and email comments on events can easily be gathered to add to a news mix of reported fact and public opinion.

Television news brings us remarkable images of events from around the world but radio news has responded in particularly interesting ways. It has been radio rather than television which has been most active in the democratisation of news through phone-ins and other forms of citizen engagement. In addition, radio's tendency to allow presenters and reporters to discuss and speculate about the news has, perhaps unintentionally, acknowledged the contested nature of 'news facts'.

FURTHER READING

Shingler and Wieringa (1998: 94–109) discuss the truth claims made by radio news in a clear and informative style. For a well researched book on international radio news and journalism see Crook (1998) and for an historical view see Nicholas (1996) on the BBC in the Second World War. Dunn's (2003) article on radio news reading is also useful and well researched.

Politics and the Public Sphere

> These are the areas of decision making in society to which radio has the potential to make a significant contribution.

The relationship between radio and politics is so complex and diverse that a single entry can do little more than point to some important historical examples and pose one or two key questions. This necessarily cursory discussion should be read in conjunction with entries on **News, Propaganda, Journalism, Hate Radio, Current Affairs** and **Talk Radio**. One way of addressing this issue is to start with the concept of the public sphere and in particular the famous discussion of it by Habermas (1989). He saw the public sphere as a space, real or virtual, where individuals could come together to discuss public affairs and reach conclusions. The modern public sphere reached its most perfect expression at the end of the 18th and beginning of the 19th centuries among the bourgeoisie, engaged in artistic and political debate in the coffee houses and salons of the time. For students of the media the theory is important because it has been a springboard for different discussions of the media and its role in politics. In the case of radio we could ask if the discussion and debate we hear on the radio is a kind of surrogate public sphere which informs our own understanding of, and participation in, politics. Do the news and current affairs programmes, mainly on public service stations, inform the electorate and stimulate political engagement? Alternatively, does radio act to peddle a political ideology? Does music radio in particular foreclose political debate with its stifling blend of consumerism and popular culture?

An interesting take on the question of political coverage on radio is offered by Andrew Crisell (2004). He suggests that television coverage of politics is largely driven by the need for visual imagery and that television more generally is mainly concerned with the visually sensational. Television illustrates political stories with images of politicians, buildings, war, crowds and so on. Radio, conversely, has an approach which 'seems somewhat more abstract, more concerned with issues and generalities in the realms of current affairs, science, ethics, feminism, the law, the arts, psychology and aesthetics, the media' (Crisell, 2004: 18). So for Crisell, radio's 'blindness' is a strength in this case and is a reason to believe that radio has a positive contribution to make to the public sphere.

The early years of radio broadcasting offer some very different examples of radio's participation in, or avoidance of, politics. The US example is interesting for the fairly uninhibited acceptance of political radio and the early direct use of radio to convey political messages. President Franklin D. Roosevelt was an enthusiastic broadcaster and used radio to address the American people directly in his 'fireside chats'. Speaking in a direct and personal manner to the listener, Roosevelt won support for his New Deal policies and American participation in the Second World War (Loviglio, 2005). A very different example of this kind of political pedagogy is Father Charles Coughlin. The 'Radio Priest' began broadcasting religious programmes for children in 1926 but soon expanded to attract an adult audience and moved from purely religious subjects to incorporate political issues. During the 1930s Coughlin became more and more outspoken, first attacking the policies of President Hoover and then launching his assault on the twin evils of communism and international banking. By the end of the decade, Coughlin, who regularly attracted audiences of over 30 million, was an apologist for the Nazis and increasingly anti-Semitic.

A more positive example of political radio at the same time in the USA is *America's Town Meeting of the Air* (1935–1956). A good example of the US version of British 'current affairs' the programme was a panel discussion in front of a large audience which was encouraged to actively participate in the show. Unscreened audience questions were used and major political issues, including race and immigration, were addressed. Transcripts of the programme were published and available for use in schools and colleges. Political programmes of this sort in the USA were attractive to broadcasters because they helped fulfil public interest obligations and acted to deter government regulation. The British equivalent, *Any Questions*, which began in 1948 was a much tamer affair but, and maybe this says something about the difference between UK and US political radio, *Any Questions* is still broadcast complete with a repeat and a follow up, *Any Answers*.

The history of British political radio is one of much greater caution compared to the USA. John Reith, the first Director General of the BBC, fought hard to have a government-imposed ban on 'controversial' content lifted in 1928. In the decade which followed, BBC political coverage skirted round the major political issues of unemployment, homelessness and the rise of fascism. Lacey describes how during the Depression years of the 1930s there was a huge increase in radio listening but the BBC saw its purpose not to provide political information but to paper over social and political divisions, 'radio was seized upon as a tool that could bind the various constituents of the nation together, wherever they were and whatever their circumstances' (2002: 29). A characteristic of the cautious approach was the absence of the voice of ordinary people, the almost universal use of scripted speech and the reluctance to address contentious issues.

The post-war BBC, buoyed up by its success and popularity during the war, began to see political coverage, both in news and current affairs programmes, as a central part of its mission. Spurred on by competition from the newly formed Independent Television (ITV) from 1955, both BBC television and radio were forced to provide a bolder and less deferential style of political coverage. Radio news magazines like *Today*, *The World at One* and *PM* provided a mix of news and comment and were more prepared to question politicians about their actions. In-depth political analysis on specialist programmes, most notably *Analysis* and *File on Four*, added to the repertoire of political coverage on BBC Radio 4 which had become the home of radio news and current affairs. In the 1970s political radio was also to be found on the newly created commercial or 'Independent Local Radio'. The first ILR station, LBC, and the commercial news service, introduced an approach which was far more innovative than the BBC and benefited from Australian and American influences (Crook, 1998: 261–81). The phone-in became an important part of the ILR schedule and this allowed callers to express their views as well as handing the microphone to presenters like Brian Hayes who had political agendas of their own. Another feature of LBC output was its parliamentary unit which, alongside the BBC, began broadcasting from parliament in 1975. Unlike the BBC, however, LBC made much more extensive use of parliamentary proceedings, including the dramatic debates at the start of the Falklands war in 1983.

Politics is not, of course, just about coverage and discussion of mainstream political processes; interviewing politicians, giving election results or discussing the musical chairs of a cabinet. Radical politics, of both left and right, has found more opportunities on radio than television. The entry on **Community Radio** describes examples of radio in the hands of organised labour, most notably the Bolivian miners' radio stations which gave a voice to the workers, their families and their trade union despite the oppression and attempted censorship of the Bolivian dictatorship. In the USA, the first signs of radical radio came with the establishment of the Pacifica Foundation in 1946 by a group of conscientious objectors, anarchists, communists and other radicals who went in 1949 to found the station KPFA in Berkeley, California. This was listener-sponsored radio which covered the arts, culture and some politics on the pre-1960s west coast. In Europe, Italian student radicals in the 1970s launched Radio Alice in Bologna which featured live reports of street demonstrations and even a riot in 1977:

> Alice was there, covering the melee – or, perhaps, allowing the melee to cover itself. Wherever police attacked, someone would grab a phone, call the studio, and go on the air. Alice became the protestors' communication system, a giant revolutionary Citizens Band, a portal open to any listener who wanted to join the revolt. (Walker, 2001: 173)

On the political right we find what is perhaps the most extraordinary and blatantly political form of radio, US **talk radio**. Susan Douglas provides vivid portrait of 'shock jocks' such as Don Imus and Howard Stern who mixed puerile rudeness with outlandishly reactionary beliefs (1999: 284–327). Talk radio was famously opposed to President Clinton's liberal health and law and order policies and brutally anti-feminist and anti-environmentalist. The shock jock was a gender activist, 'an ideological soldier in the war to reassert patriarchy' (1999: 317). In a fascinating piece of analysis, Douglas points out that talk radio became important at the same time that National Public Radio became more established and politically and culturally significant. NPR and talk radio were poles apart in 'almost every imaginable way' but they can both be seen as a response to the failures of mainstream radio. People felt excluded from the public sphere, they wanted a space, a surrogate public sphere which is what NPR and talk radio offered:

> They both became electronic surrogates for the town common, the village square, the general store, the meeting hall, the coffee house, the beer garden, the park, where people imagined their grandparents – even their parents for that matter – might have gathered with others to chat, however briefly, about the state of the town, the country, the world. NPR and political talk radio both tapped into the sense of loss of public life in the 1980s and beyond, the isolation that came from overwork and the privatization

of American life, and the huge gap people felt between themselves and those who run the country. (Douglas, 1999: 285)

Habermas (1989) saw the public sphere as the bridge between the individual and the state, between the private and the public. The mass media has played its part in the fall of the public sphere and in particular through a process of 'dumbing down' as commercial media goes in pursuit of the widest audience. And yet community radio, public service radio and, if we are to believe Douglas, even talk radio have played their part in reinstating surrogate opportunities for political engagement.

FURTHER READING

The bolder student will want to have a look at the work of Habermas (1989) in the original but there are also some very good accounts of his central ideas online. Crisell (2004) makes some interesting points about politics and radio. For a history of American radio and the public sphere see Loviglio (2005). Lacey (2002) provides a good summary and analysis of the BBC in the 1930s and Douglas (1999: 284–327) on talk radio is a fascinating read.

Propaganda

> *Media messages designed to indoctrinate or influence listeners by providing distorted or one-sided information.*

The word propaganda can be traced back to 1622 when Pope Gregory XV established the Sacred Congregation for the Propagation of the Faith, a body designed to propagate the teachings and orthodoxy of the church. In the last century, the word propaganda was associated with political movements and in particular the propaganda of Nazi Germany and the Soviet Union. It refers to the use of one-sided and selective information, often couched in dramatic language or imagery, designed to influence or indoctrinate people. It is worth observing that the rise of the systematic use of propaganda in the first half of the 20th century coincided with the emergence of radio as a medium of mass communication and radio had an important part to play in early propagandist campaigns.

Nazi propaganda was directed by Joseph Goebbels who identified the need to produce propaganda at home to ensure the conformity of the population and to maintain morale during the war, but also abroad where it can be used as an instrument of war. A good example of the latter was the German offensive against Austria. Before Germany invaded Austria in 1938, radio propaganda was used to gain support for Nazi policies and 100,000 radio sets were distributed in Austria to encourage listening.

Perhaps the most famous example of using propaganda against the enemy's civilian population is the case of William Joyce, 'Lord Haw-Haw'. Joyce broadcast to the British population from Radio Hamburg his messages designed to weaken morale and exaggerate the success of the German war machine. Joyce's broadcasts coincided with the beginnings of BBC research into radio listening which revealed that a remarkable 27 per cent of the British population tuned in to Radio Hamburg after the BBC's *Nine O'Clock News* (Street, 2006a: 191). They would probably have been entertained more than indoctrinated on hearing that, 'Famine stalks side by side with Winston Churchill today. England will become a land of skeletons by the wayside ...' (quoted in Hickman, 1995: 35). There may have been an illicit thrill in listening to the sneering voice of Haw-Haw but his popularity was a sharp reminder to the BBC of its own failings. The solution came in the form of the morale raising *Postscripts* delivered by the great wartime broadcaster J.B. Priestley at exactly the same time that people were switching over the Hamburg.

Winston Churchill was also a famous broadcaster and his morale-raising speeches if not propaganda were certainly designed to use radio to help in the war effort. The hasty evacuation of British forces from the beaches of Dunkirk was an ignominious moment but one which was brilliantly turned by Churchill into a rallying cry:

> We shall go on to the end ... we shall fight on the seas and oceans, we shall fight with growing confidence and growing strength in the air, we shall defend our island whatever the cost might be. We shall fight on the beaches, we shall fight on the landing grounds, we shall fight in the fields and in the streets. We shall never surrender. (Quoted in Hickman, 1995: 34)

In her analysis of BBC radio in the Second World War, Nicholas argues that radio was 'the most important institution of communication during the war' (1996: 4). There were two reasons for this: first, the BBC had a good reputation for being a reliable and professional, if slightly dull, source of news; and, second:

> ... the nature of radio itself was a crucial factor. Because of the scope of its appeal, the range of presentation styles it offered and its sheer ubiquity, radio was a propaganda disseminator of vast potential. (Nicholas, 1996: 5)

BBC radio in Britain during the war was an immensely successful instrument of propaganda because of the privileged place of the BBC and radio in people's lives. Radio audiences were huge, listening was often conducted in family groups and the BBC had a large force of highly talented producers and scriptwriters to build and maintain national morale. It did this while telling some, if not all, of the truth about the progress of the war and maintaining the difficult balancing act between the government and itself.

The US experience of propaganda was different in may ways, and still is. A tradition of extreme right-wing political figures using radio to propagandise has existed almost since the start of radio broadcasting. The notorious anti-Semitic propagandist Father Charles Coughlin used radio to express his virulent and extreme views in the 1930s. This use of radio to attack sections of society and whip up prejudice and intolerance was partly restricted by the FCC and its Fairness Doctrine which made radio stations provide a more balanced political coverage. After the demise of the doctrine under President Reagan, right-wing propaganda once again became a feature of American radio. Whole stations were taken over by extreme right-wing groups including survivalists, neo-Nazis, fundamentalist Christians and conspiracy theorists. After the Oklahoma bombing in 1995 most of these groups deserted analogue radio for the Internet but the phenomenon of **talk radio** arguably allows right-wing bigots to use radio as a propaganda medium.

The USA has also been an important source of propaganda radio beamed to other parts of the world. During the Cold War, Radio Liberty broadcast into the USSR and Radio Free Europe to Eastern Europe. Similarly Radio Swan was aimed at Cuba and Radio Quince de Septiembre broadcast to Nicaragua. Voice of America has broadcast with the aim of representing American views and policies to the rest of the world since 1942. Each week it reaches over 80 million listeners in 53 languages. In the same way, the BBC World Service, financed not by the licence fee but by the British Government's Foreign Office, also represents a positive gloss on Britain. To take just one further example, Voice of Vietnam, the state-run radio of Vietnam provides both a short wave and an Internet-based radio service. Whether any of these are propaganda is open to debate, they all provide a global radio voice for the governments and policies of their countries which are at least a positive 'spin' on those if not a form of indoctrination.

Radio, as the lessons of history, and in particular the Second World War, tell us, has great potential as a medium of propaganda. The combination of the intimacy that radio can achieve with its audience and the trust which the population may, mistakenly, give it, can produce an effective mix for purposes of indoctrination. One of the most tragic examples of this was the use of radio during the Rwanda genocide of 1994 (see the entry on **Hate Radio**). Broadcasts by Radio-Télévision Libre des Milles Collines encouraged the Hutus to slaughter one million of their fellow Tutsis. This was the phenomenon of hate radio and a form of the most extreme and deadly radio propaganda. A reminder of the terrible power of the medium to influence listeners.

FURTHER READING

There are two excellent accounts of radio propaganda during the Second World War: Nicholas (1996) and Hickman (1995). For a look at the American example see Keith and Hill (2004) on hate radio.

Public Service Broadcasting

> *A broadcasting model epitomised by the BBC and which gives priority to serving the public with a mix of information, education and entertainment.*

It is possible to categorise all radio on the basis of the way it is funded and the motives of those who produce it. Hendy has suggested that there are five categories of radio which can be identified as:

State radio;
Underground (or free or pirate) radio;
Community radio;
Commercial radio;
Public Service Radio. (2000: 14)

It is the last category which concerns us here and which has proved to be extremely difficult to define. Public Service Radio, unlike State radio, is not directly controlled by the state although it is often partly reliant on state funding. It is most likely to be found in parliamentary democracies and Hendy cites as good examples NHK (the Broadcasting Corporation of Japan) in Japan, Canada's CBC (Canadian Broadcasting Corporation) and, most famously of all, the British Broadcasting Corporation (BBC). In the USA, National Public Radio (NPR) is a variant on the public service model and worth thinking about at the same time.

It is hard to write about Public Service Broadcasting (PSB) without writing a history essay. The idea of public service and its application to radio broadcasting are deeply rooted in the history of the BBC and its Victorian (or 19th century) antecedents. PSB may well be history in another sense; its days may be numbered in the new multimedia environment in which choice is king.

Historians of PSB trace it back to the writings of Matthew Arnold in 19th-century Britain. Arnold, whose views had a great influence on the first Director General of the BBC, John Reith, believed that culture could alleviate social divisions and prevent anarchy. Like many writers of his time and in the following decades, Arnold was afraid of the dangers of the masses and saw the civilising potential of culture and education.

The British government in the early 1920s saw the potential of the newly formed BBC to influence the views of the population and so set up the Sykes Committee to consider all aspects of broadcasting and what its uses might be. The committee's report defined broadcasting as a 'public utility' (as opposed to a commercial operation) which would be a national service in the public interest. Over the next few years, Reith, influenced by not only Arnold but his own evangelical Christianity, patriotism and moral authoritarianism (Avery, 2006: 15) set about turning these rather vague ambitions into broadcasting policy. The authority of the early BBC was greatly enhanced by the granting of a Royal Charter in 1926 and the creation from the beginning of 1927 of the BBC as a corporation, answerable only to parliament. As Scannell and Cardiff put it, the Charter was the BBC's 'passport into the state domain' (1991: 40). But what did all of this mean in terms of programming? The early BBC strove for the highest possible standards of output which meant that the 'great and the good' were invited to speak on the radio and the schedule was full of worthy cultural and religious content. At the same time Reith wanted to reach the widest possible audience and so PSB was not just education and information, it was also entertainment. A policy of mixed programming meant that dance bands and comics could be heard on the BBC, but these were interspersed with serious radio talks and classical concerts.

For a variety of reasons this rather stuffy and patronising approach began to change as those who ran the BBC realised it was out of touch with its listeners and perceived as giving people what they needed rather than what they wanted. Some of the main factors contributing to change were that Reith left the BBC just before the Second World War, a populist, commercial radio service was successfully beamed into the UK from the continent and then the war itself forced a serious look at programming for all social classes. BBC radio was divided after the war into three separate 'networks': the Home Service; the Third Programme; and the Light Programme. This rationalisation articulated two challenges to the earlier PSB orthodoxy. Elite cultural output was separated out (in the Third Programme) and 'light entertainment' including dance music, soaps and quizzes given its own network. The working class was far less likely to experience the civilising effect of high culture if it was tuned only to the Light Programme. And yet the BBC, in both its radio and television policies and output, continued to be heavily influenced by the ideals of PSB, as one writer has articulated it:

> Public [service] broadcasting is above all else ... a belief that the sheer presence of broadcasting within all our lives can and must be used to nurture society, to proffer the opportunity for society and its inhabitants to be better served than by systems which primarily seek consumers for advertisers. (Tracey, 1998: 18)

Although the core values of public service broadcasting were changed and to a degree weakened in the BBC in the second part of the last century, the corporation maintained its commitment to public service values including cultural breadth and quality, originality in drama and factual programming and impartiality in news and current affairs. The BBC's director general during the 1960s, Hugh Greene, presided over a decade of radical and innovative output which he saw as part of the public service remit:

> I see it as the clear duty of a public service broadcasting organization to stand firm against attempts to decry sincerity and vision – we have a duty to take account of the changes in society, to be ahead of public opinion, rather than always to wait upon it. I believe that great broadcasting organisations, with their immense powers of patronage of writers and artisans, should not neglect to cultivate young writers who may, by any, be considered 'too advanced' or 'shocking'. (Greene, quoted in Tracey, 1998: xi)

The principles of public service are still alive in what Georgina Born has called 'the world's most famous cultural institution', the BBC (2004: 5). It is still true that the licence fee, a form of direct taxation which nets the corporation several billions of pounds a year, is its main source of revenue, thus freeing it from the pressures of commercialism. The commitment to high quality and original programming is still present as is the nationalistic marking of British, and especially royal and sporting, events. But the very notion of 'public service' now looks very dated and even broadcasting to mass audiences is in decline. Both the neo-liberal market policies of Margaret Thatcher (Prime Minister from 1979–1990) which encouraged commercial competition, and the huge increase in consumer choice as a result of the digital revolution, have weakened PSB in Britain.

Before considering how PSB has survived in the UK, and how it might survive in other parts of the world, let us turn to the US equivalent, NPR. Although US radio is widely seen as highly commercial there has always been a tradition of university and college-based stations whose goals and programming are at least reminiscent of PSB. In the 1920s a number of educational public service stations existed mainly based in schools and colleges. Few of these survived the Depression in the 1930s but after the war the Federal Communications Commission allotted 20 of the new FM channels to educational broadcasters. The main driver for US public service radio was the Public Broadcasting Act 1967 which led to the establishment of National Public Radio. NPR grew from university roots and many of the early participants were former students activists (Mitchell, 2002: 413). Karl Schmidy from the University of

Wisconsin station at Madison was a member of the NPR's founding board and advocated radio based on the lives of 'real people' that allowed 'ideas and experiences to be shared, considered and modified' (Mitchell, 2002: 413). This was to be a decentralised, democratic, inclusive radio which brought to the microphone all races, regions and ideologies. Another founding board member, Bill Siemering, had ambitions for radio Matthew Arnold himself might have agreed with:

> National Public Radio ... will regard the individual differences among men with respect and joy rather than derision and hate; it will celebrate the human experience as infinitely varied rather than vacuous and banal; it will encourage a sense of active constructive participation, rather than apathetic helplessness ...

> The programs will enable the individual to better understand himself, his government, is institutions, and his national and social environment so he can intelligently participate in effecting the process of change... (Mitchell, 2002: 414)

Today, NPR produces 100 hours of programming a week for its 600 member stations. These include the well respected drive-time news magazines *Morning Edition* and *All Things Considered*. Over on the alternative network, American Public Radio still produces the most popular programme on public radio, Garrison Keillor's *Prairie Home Companion*. Perhaps the most important contribution made by public service radio in the USA has been in its news coverage. Tiananmen Square, the Persian Gulf and Iraq wars, the fall of the Berlin Wall alongside its award-winning political and legal coverage have all added to its reputation. That having been said, public radio in the USA remains a niche activity and nowhere near as widely listened to, or as influential, as BBC radio. Whether that is a good or a bad thing is very much a matter of opinion.

It would be wrong at this point to heave a collective sigh for the golden days of public service radio with its quality, impartiality and innovation and commitment to something other than profit and to think that it has no place in the modern world. In the epilogue to her important book on the BBC, Born warns us of the perils of the multichannel and Internet worlds. Global media tends to be dominated by genres that easily cross cultural boundaries – sport, Hollywood movies, pop music and pornography. Migrant and minority communities may also retreat into experiencing idealised representations of their homeland provided by satellite television. As for the Internet, it poses the threat of an unending supply of unsubstantiated information or rumour. But against this backdrop public service broadcasting, has an extremely important role to play. It can be a place where all social groups can be heard. Where the voice of the minority is not confined to an obscure web site or station, but is placed in the public sphere and heard by us all (BBC radio's Asian network is a good example of this). In addition, the Internet is often seen as a challenge to PSB but it can also provide an important opportunity. The BBC's huge and much-praised web site brings a degree of impartiality and trust to 'what can otherwise be, for many users, simply the noise of the net' (Born, 2004: 514).

FURTHER READING

For further reading on American public service radio a good starting place would be Flinthoff (2004) or Mitchell (2002). British public service radio, in the form of the BBC, is particularly well examined by Tracey (1998) but both Hendy (2000) and Born (2004) are full of insights. Interestingly, the celebrated BBC website (http://www. bbc.co.uk) is also an expression of public service values.

Radiocracy

Radiocracy refers to radio's unique contribution to participatory democracy.

The relationship between radio and democracy has been usefully captured in a term originally coined by Hartley (2000). It refers to the ability of radio, and in particular public service and community forms, to contribute to the public sphere. Hartley suggests that radio can contribute to community building and provides a low-cost and low-tech public space. Community radio is obviously well positioned to provide this democratic intervention as he explains rhetorically:

How does a community define itself as such? What connects its members to the 'imagined community' of modern associated life? What links that community to its representative bodies, and to the world at large? How do smaller groups, especially remote, marginal, disenfranchised or oppressed communities, press for their place among others? (Hartley, 2000: 154)

In this early discussion of the concept, Hartley quotes Brecht who in Germany in the 1920s saw radio's potential to contribute to democracy. Radio could help citizens engage actively in the public sphere by broadcasting interviews and discussions. With extraordinary foresight, Brecht argued that radio could only fulfil its radiocratic potential if there was some interactivity between radio and its audience. Although his idea of interactivity was very different from the one we use today, the growth of radio phone-ins and contributing emails and texts do seem to prove his point.

The word 'radiocracy' was given greater prominence in two international conferences which bore its name; one in Cardiff, UK, in 1999 and the other in Durban, South Africa, in 2001. The second of these conferences probably owed its existence to Thabo Mbeki, the President of South Africa, who had taken the view that in post-Apartheid South Africa radio had an important role as a tool for creating democracy out of the previous police state. In the 1990s, Mbeki had encouraged the use of radio, and especially as a two-way medium attentive to the views of its audience, in the democratic process. This was particularly appropriate in a country with very low literacy rates.

The idea that radio contributes to the political process is of course hardly new. It is enshrined in the very notion of **public service broadcasting**, although there are plenty of examples in American commercial radio of democratic discussion and debate. The main advocate for the radiocratric nature of public service radio has been Scannell. His account of public service broadcasting and modern public life contains these words:

> I wish to argue for broadcasting in its present form, as a public good that has unobtrusively contributed to the democratisation of everyday life, in public and private contest, from its beginning through to today. (Scannell, 1992: 317)

Scannell argues forcefully that by bringing politicians and political debate to the microphone, the BBC had a powerful, if flawed, democratic influence on 20th century Britain. It is interesting to note that for both Scannell and Hartley, the radiocratic nature of radio was not simply a political phenomenon (as in news and current affairs). The introduction of the general public to cultural events and entertainment, impossible before the invention of radio, also had a democratising function, 'by placing political, religious, civic, cultural events and entertainments in a common domain, public life was equalised in a way that had never before been possible' (Scannell, 1992: 317).

Not everyone would agree that radio has the special relationship with democracy that the term radiocracy implies. Radio can also be the enemy of democracy when its function has been to indoctrinate as it did in Nazi Germany or during the Rwandan genocide (see the entries on **Propaganda** and **Hate Radio**). Community radio can be genuinely radiocratic but it too often loses sight of its original goals. Well intentioned community radio which makes an important contribution to the public sphere can quite easily be diverted from its mission. In a culturally diverse community who is the community station speaking for? Also, if there are a few enthusiasts running a station there is the danger that they become entrenched and the rest of the community is excluded (Hendy, 2000: 199). Successful community radio stations also run the risk of being taken over or 'professionalised' as happened at KPFA at Berkeley, California, which went from being a station opposed to the Korean War and for the legalisation of cannabis in the 1950s to just another part of the media mainstream (Walker, 2001: 159–61).

FURTHER READING

As this is such an undeveloped concept it is unsurprising that the reading is so thin. The essential text is a rather cursory statement, important nonetheless, by Hartley 2000). Of relevance, although without using the term 'radiocracy', is Scannell's (1992) extremely important statement about public service broadcasting.

radiocracy

references

Adams, M. and Phipp, S. (2004) 'Low-power radio/microradio', in C. Sterling (ed.), *The Museum of Broadcast Communications Encyclopedia of Radio*, Vol. 2. New York: Fitzroy Dearborn. pp. 885–7.

Albarran, A. (2004) 'Clear Channel Communications Inc.', in C. Sterling (ed.), *The Museum of Broadcast Communications Encyclopedia of Radio*, Volume 1. New York: Fitzroy Dearborn. p. 341.

Algan, E. (2005) 'The role of Turkish local radio in the construction of a youth community', *The Radio Journal: International Studies in Broadcast and Audio Media*, 3 (2): 75–92.

Alia, V. (2004) 'Indigenous radio in Canada', in A. Crisell (ed.), *More than a Music Box: Radio Cultures and Communities in a Multi-media World*. New York: Berghahn Books. pp. 77–94.

Anderson, B. (1983) *Imagined Communities*. London: Verso.

Anderson, S. (2004) 'Internet radio: delivering radio programs online', in C. Sterling (ed.), *The Museum of Broadcast Communications Encyclopedia of Radio*, Volume 2. New York: Fitzroy Dearborn. pp. 756–8.

Atkinson, K. and Moores, S. (2003) '"We all have bad days". Attending to face in broadcast troubles talk', *The Radio journal: International Studies in Broadcast and Audio Media*, 1 (2): 129–46.

Avery, T. (2006) *Radio Modernism: Literature, Ethics, and the BBC, 1922–1938*. Aldershot: Ashgate.

Barnard, S. (2000) *Studying Radio*. London: Arnold.

Barnett, S. and Seymour, E. (1999) *A Shrinking Iceberg Travelling South, Changing Trends in British Television: a case study of drama and current affairs*. London: Campaign for Quality Television.

Bassett, C. (2003) 'How many movements?', in M. Bull and L. Black (eds), *The Auditory Culture Reader*. Oxford: Berg. pp. 343–355.

Berry, R. (2006) 'Will the iPod kill the radio star? Profiling podcasting as radio', *Convergence*, 12 (2): 143–62.

Born, G. (2004) *Uncertain Vision: Birt, Dyke and the reinvention of the BBC*. London: Secker and Warburg.

Brand, G. and Scannell, P. (1991) 'Talk, identity and performance: The Tony Blackburn Show', in P. Scannell (ed.), *Broadcast Talk*. London: Sage. pp. 201–26.

Brendon, P. (2000) *The Dark Valley: A Panorama of the 1930s*. London: Jonathan Cape.

Bull, M. (2005) 'No dead air. The iPod and the culture of mobile listening', *Leisure Studies*, 24 (4): 343–55.

Bull, M. and Back, L. (eds) (2003) *The Auditory Culture Reader*. Oxford: Berg.

Carver, R. (2000) 'Broadcasting and political transition', in R. Fardon and G. Furniss (eds), *African Broadcast Cultures*. Oxford: James Currey. pp. 188–97.

Chignell, H. (2007) 'The London Broadcasting Company/Independent Radio News archive', *Twentieth Century British History*, 18 (4): 514–25.

Chignell, H. and Devlin, J. (2007) 'John Peel's "Home Truths"', *The Radio Journal: International Studies in Broadcast and Audio Media*, 4 (1): 69–81.

Crisell, A. (1994) *Understanding Radio*, 2nd edn. London: Routledge.

Crisell, A. (ed.) (2004) *More than a Music Box: Radio Cultures and Communities in a Multi-media W.* New York: Berghahn Books.

Crook, T. (1998) *International Radio Journalism*. London: Routledge.

Crook, T. (1999) *Radio Drama: Theory and Practice*. London: Routledge.

Dang, T. (2008) 'Radio and its listenership in the Internet age: a case study of Voice of Vietnam and Voice of Vietnam News', unpublished PhD thesis, Bournemouth University.

Donovan, P. (1998) *All Our Todays: Forty Years of the* Today *Programme*. London: Arrow Books.

Douglas, S. (1999) *Listening In: Radio and the American Imagination, from Amos 'n' Andy and Edward R. Murrow to Wolfman Jack and Howard Stern*. New York: Random House.

Dunn, A. (2003) 'Telling the story: narrative and radio news', *The Radio Journal: International Studies in Broadcast and audio Media*, 1 (2): 113–27.

Ellis, E. and Shane, E. (2004) 'Talk radio', in C. Sterling (ed.), *The Museum of Broadcast Communications Encyclopedia of Radio*, Vol. 3. New York: Fitzroy Dearborn. pp. 1369–74.

Ellis, J. (2000) *Seeing Things*. London: I. B. Tauris.

Ellis, S.L. (2004) 'Transistor radios', in C. Sterling (ed.), *The Museum of Broadcast Communications Encyclopedia of Radio*, Vol. 3. New York: Fitzroy Dearborn. pp. 1413–14.

Everett, (1999) *www.jiscmail.ac.uk*. Radio Studies, 1 March.

Fardon, R. and Furniss, G. (eds) (2000) *African Broadcast Cultures*. Oxford: James Currey.

Flintoff, C. (2004) 'National Public Radio', in C. Sterling (ed.), *The Museum of Broadcast Communications Encyclopedia of Radio*, Vol. 2. New York: Fitzroy Dearborn. pp. 1000–6.

Franklin, B., Hamer, M., Hanna, M., Kinsey, M. and Richardson, J. (2005) *Key Concepts in Journalism Studies*. London: Sage.

Garner, K. (1993) *In Session Tonight: The Complete Radio 1 Recordings*. London: BBC Books.

Gilliam, L. (1950) *BBC Features*. London: Evans Brothers.

Gordon, J. (2006) 'A comparison of a sample of new British community radio stations with a parallel sample of established Australian community radio stations', *3C Media, Journal of Community, Citizen's and Third Sector Media and Communication* 2: pp. 1–16.

Gray, F. (2004) 'Fireside issues: audience, listener, soundscape', in A. Crisell (ed.), *More than a Music Box: Radio Cultures and Communities in a Multi-media World*. New York: Berghahn Books. pp. 247–62.

Habermas, J. (1989) *Structural Transformation of the Public Sphere*. Cambridge: Polity.

Harman, J. 2004) 'Recording and studio equipment', in C. Sterling (ed.) *The Museum of Broadcast Communications Encyclopedia of Radio*, Vol. 3. New York: Fitzroy Dearborn. pp. 1187–93.

Hartley, J. (2000) 'Radiocracy: sound and citizenship', *International journal of Cultural Studies*, 3 (2): 153–9.

Haworth, J. (2000) 'Women in radio news: making a difference?', in C. Mitchell (ed.), *Women and Radio: Airing differences*. London: Routledge. pp. 250–61.

Hendy, D. (2004) '"Reality radio": the documentary', in A. Crisell (ed.), *More than a Music Box: Radio Cultures and Communities in a Multi-media World*. New York: Berghahn Books. pp. 167–88.

Hendy, D. (2000) *Radio in the Global Age*. London: Polity Press.

Hendy, D. (2007) *Life on Air: A History of Radio Four*. Oxford: Oxford University Press.

Hickman, T. (1995) *What Did You Do in the War, Auntie?* London: BBC Books.

Higgins, C.S. and Moss, P.D. (1982) *Sounds Real: Radio and Everyday Life*. St Lucia: University of Queensland Press.

Hilliard, H.L. and Keith, M.C. (2005) *The Quieted Voice: The Rise and Demise of Localism in American Radio*. Carbondale, IL: Southern Illinois University Press.

Hilmes, M. (1997) *Radio Voices: American Broadcasting, 1922–1952*. Minneapolis, MN: University of Minnesota Press.

Hilmes, M. and Loviglio, J. (eds) (2002) *Radio Reader: Essays in the Cultural History of Radio*. New York: Routledge.

Holland, P. (2006) *The Angry Buzz: 'This Week' and Current Affairs Television*. London: I.B. Tauris.

Hutchby, I. (1991) 'The organization of talk on talk radio', in P. Scannell (ed.), *Broadcast Talk*. London: Sage. pp. 119–38.

Jallov, B. (2005) 'Assessing community change: development of a 'bare foot' impact assessment methodology', *The Radio Journal: International Studies in Broadcast and Audio Media*, 3 (1): 21–34.

Kang, S. (2004) 'Fairness Doctrine: controversial issue broadcasting policy', in C. Sterling (ed.), *The Museum of Broadcast Communications Encyclopedia of Radio*, Vol. 2. New York: Fitzroy Dearborn. pp. 563–6.

Keith, M. (2004) 'Norman Corwin', in C. Sterling (ed.), *The Museum of Broadcast Communications Encyclopedia of Radio*, Vol. 1. New York: Fitzroy Dearborn. pp. 405–8.

Keith, M. and Hilliard, R. (2004) 'Hate radio', in C. Sterling (ed.), *The Museum of Broadcast Communications Encyclopedia of Radio*, Vol. 2. New York: Fitzroy Dearborn. pp. 694–5.

Keith, M. and Sterling, C. (2004) 'Disc jockeys;, in C.H. Sterling (ed.), *Encyclopedia of Radio*. New York: Fitzroy Dearborn. pp. 471–3.

Kelly Huff, W. and Sterling, C. (2004) 'AM Radio' , in C. Sterling, (ed.) *The Museum of Broadcast Communications Encyclopedia of Radio*, Volume 1. New York: Fitzroy Dearborn: 83-85.

Lacey, K. (2002) 'Radio in the Great Depression: promotional culture, public service and propaganda', in M. Hilmes and J. Loviglio (eds), *Radio Reader: Essays in the Cultural History of Radio*. New York: Routledge. pp. 21–40.

Land, J. (1999) *Active Radio: Pacifica's brash experiment*. Minneapolis: University of Minnesota Press.

Lewis, P. (2004) 'Opening and closing doors: radio drama in the BBC', *The Radio Journal: International Studies in Broadcast and Audio Media*, 1 (3): 161–76.

Ligaga, D. (2005 'Enacting the quotidian in Kenyan radio drama: "Not Now" and the narrative of forced marriage', *The Radio Journal: International Studies in Broadcast and Audio Media*, 3 (2): 107–19.

Limburg, V. (2004) 'Murrow, Edward R. 1908–1965' in C. Sterling (ed.), *The Museum of Broadcast Communications Encyclopedia of Radio*, Vol. 2. New York: Fitzroy Dearborn. pp. 966–9.

Linfoot, M. (2007) 'Voices–sharing unheard stories on BBC Local Radio', *The Radio Journal: International Studies in Broadcast and Audio Media*, 4 (1–3): 125–40.

Lockyer, S. and Pickering, M. (2005) *Beyond a Joke: The Limits of Humour.* Basingstoke: Palgrave Macmillan.

Long, P. (2006) 'The primary code: the meanings of John Peel, radio and popular music', *The Radio journal: International Studies in Broadcast and Audio Media*, 4 (1–3): 25–48.

Loviglio, J. (2005) *Radio's Intimate Public: Network Broadcasting and Mass-Mediated Democracy.* Minneapolis, MN: University of Minnesota Press.

MacFarland, D.T. (1997) *Future Radio Programming Strategies: Cultivating Listenership in the Digital Age.* Mahwah, NJ: Lawrence Erlbaum.

Mano, W. (2005) 'Scheduling for rural and urban listeners on bilingual Radio Zimbabwe', *The Radio Journal: International Studies in Broadcast and Audio Media*, 3 (2): 93–106.

Mason, M. (1971) *The Listener*, 18 November 1971, quoted in D. Hendy (2007) *Life On Air: A History of Radio Four.* Oxford: Oxford University Press.

McLuhan, M. (1994) *Understanding Media: The Extensions of Man.* Boston, MA: MIT Press.

Mitchell, C. (ed.) (2000) *Women and Radio: Airing Differences.* London: Routledge.

Mitchell, J. (2002) 'Lead us not into temptation: American public radio in a world of infinite possibilities', in M. Hilmes and J. Loviglio (eds), *Radio Reader: Essays in the Cultural History of Radio.* New York: Routledge. pp. 405–22.

Montgomery, M. (1986) 'DJ talk', *Media, Culture and Society*, 8: 421–40.

Moore, P. (2003) 'Legacy. Fourth phase public service broadcasting in Northern Ireland', *The Radio Journal: International Studies in Broadcast and Audio Media*, 2 (1): 87–100.

Murray, M. (2002) '"The Tendency to Deprave and Corrupt Morals" Regulation and irregular sexuality in golden age radio comedy', in M. Hilmes and J. Loviglio (eds), *Radio Reader: Essays in the Cultural History of Radio.* New York: Routledge. pp. 135–56.

Murray Shafer, R. (2003) 'Open Ears' in M. Bull and L. Black (eds), *The Auditory Culture Reader.* Oxford: Berg. pp. 25–39.

Myers, M. (2000) 'Community radio and development: issues and examples from Francophone West Africa', in R. Fardon and G. Furniss (eds), *African Broadcast Cultures.* Oxford: James Currey. pp. 90–101.

Mytton, G. (2004) 'Africa', in C. Sterling (ed.), *The Museum of Broadcast Communications Encyclopedia of Radio*, Vol. 1. New York: Fitzroy Dearborn. pp. 17–22.

Nicholas, S. (1996) *The Echo of War: Home Front Proaganda and the Wartime BBC, 1939–45.* Manchester: Manchester University Press.

O'Connor, A. (ed.) (2004) *Community Radio in Bolivia: The Miners' Radio Stations.* Lewiston: The Edwin Mellen Press.

Ofcom (Office of Communications) (2004) *Radio–Preparing for the Future, Phase 1: Developing a New Framework.* London: Office of Communications.

Ong, W. (1988) *Orality and Literacy.* London: Routledge

Peel, J. and Ravenscroft, S. (2005) *Margrave of the Marshes.* London: Bantam Press.

Priestman, C. (2002) *Web Radio: Radio Production for Internet Streaming*. Oxford: Focal Press.

Radway, J. (1991) *Reading the Romance*. Chapter Hill: University of North Carolina Press.

Riismandel, P. (2002) 'Radio by and for the public: the death and resurrection of low-power radio', in M. Hilmes and J. Loviglio (eds), *Radio Reader: Essays in the Cultural History of Radio*. New York: Routledge. pp 423–50.

Rothenbuhler, E. and McCourt, T. (2002) 'Radio redefines itself, 1947–1962', in M. Hilmes and J. Loviglio (eds), *Radio Reader: Essays in the Cultural History of Radio*. New York: Routledge. pp. 367–88.

Scannell, P. (1991) *Broadcast Talk*. London: Sage.

Scannell, P. (1992) 'Public service broadcasting and modern public life', in P. Scannell, P. Schlesinger and C. Sparks (eds) *Culture and Power: A Media Culture an Society Reader*. London: Sage.

Scannell, P. (1996) *Radio, Television and Modern Life*. Oxford: Blackwell.

Scannell, P. (2007) *Media and Communication*. London: Sage.

Scannell, P. and Cardiff, D. (1991) *A Social History of British Broadcasting, Volume 1: 1922–1939*. Oxford: Blackwell.

Shingler, M. and Wieringa, C. (1998) *On Air: Methods and Meanings of Radio*. London: Arnold.

Skues, K. (1994) *Pop Went the Pirates*. Sheffield: Lamb's Meadow Publications.

Smith, B.R. (2003) 'Tuning into London c.1600', in M. Bull and L. Back (eds), *The Auditory Culture Reader*. Oxford: Berg. pp. 127–35.

Smith, J.E. (2002) 'Radio's "cultural front", 1938–1948', in M. Hilmes and J. Loviglio (eds), *Radio Reader: Essays in the Cultural History of Radio*. New York: Routledge. pp. 209–30.

Smulyan, S. (1994) *Selling Radio: The Commercialization of American Broadcasting 1920–1934*. Washington, DC: Smithsonian Institution Press.

Starkey, G. (2004a) *Radio in Context*. Basingstoke: Palgrave Macmillan.

Starkey, G. (2004b) 'BBC Radio 5 Live: extending choice through "Radio Bloke"?', in A. Crisell (ed.), *More than a Music Box: Radio Cultures and Communities in a Multi-media World*. New York: Berghahn Books. pp. 21–38.

Stearn, G.E. (1968) *McLuhan: Hot and Cool*. London: Penguin Books.

Sterling, C. (ed.) (2004a) *The Museum of Broadcast Communications Encyclopedia of Radio*, Vols 1–3. New York: Fitzroy Dearborn.

Sterling, C. (2004b) 'FM radio' in C. Sterling (ed.), *The Museum of Broadcast Communications Encyclopedia of Radio*, Vol. 2. New York: Fitzroy Dearborn. pp. 602–8.

Sterling, C. (2004c) 'Receivers', in C. Sterling (ed.), *The Museum of Broadcast Communications Encyclopedia of Radio*, Vol. 3. New York: Fitzroy Dearborn. pp. 1183–7.

Street, S. (2002) *A Concise History of British Radio, 1922–2002*. Tiverton: Kelly.

Street, S. (2004) 'Programme-makers on Parker: occupational reflections on the radio production legacy of Charles Parker', *The Radio Journal: International Studies in Broadcast and Audio Media*, 2 (3): 187–194.

Street, S. (2006a) *Crossing the Ether: British Public Service Radio and Commercial Competition 1922–1945*. Eastleigh: John Libbey.

Street, S. (2006b) *Historical Dictionary of British Radio*. Lanham, MD: The Scarecrow Press.

Tacchi, J. (2003) 'Nostalgia and radio sound', in M. Bull and L. Back (eds), *The Auditory Culture Reader*. Oxford: Berg. pp. 281–95.

Taylor-McCain, J. (2007) 'Pre-war radio development and design', Centre for Broadcasting History Research, Bournemouth University lecture series, 1 March.

Terrence Gordon, W. (1997) *Marshall McLuhan: Escape into Understanding, a Biography.* New York: Basic Books.

Thibaud, J. (2003) 'The sonic composition of the city', in M. Bull and L. Back (eds), *The Auditory Culture Reader.* Oxford: Berg. pp. 329–41.

Thompson, E. (2004) *The Soundscape of Modernity: Architectural Acoustics and the Culture of Listening in America, 1900–1933.* Cambridge, MA: MIT Press.

Thumin, J. (2004 *Inventing Television Culture: Men, Women and the Box.* Oxford: Oxford University Press.

Tolson, A. (2006) *Media Talk: Spoken Discourse on TV and Radio.* Edinburgh: Edinburgh University Press.

Tracey, M. (1998) *The Decline and Fall of Public Service Broadcasting.* Oxford: Oxford University Press.

van Selm, M., Jankowski, N. and Kleijn, B. (2004) 'Dutch web radio as a medium for audience interaction', in A. Crisell (ed.), *More than a Music Box: Radio Cultures and Communities in a Multi-media World.* New York: Berghahn. pp. 265–82.

Wagg, S. (ed.) (1998) *Because I Tell a Joke or Two: Comedy, Politics and Social Difference.* London: Routledge.

Walker, J. (2001) *Rebels on the Air: An Alternative History of Radio in America.* New York: New York University Press.

Wall, M. (2004) *John Peel.* London: Orion.

Wall, T. (2004) 'The political economy of Internet music radio', *The Radio Journal: International Studies in Broadcast and Audio Media*, 2 (1): 27–44.

Williams, R. (1974) *Television: Technology and Cultural Form.* London: Fontana.

references